About the

Chris Waterlow was born in London and educated at Stonyhurst College in Lancashire. On leaving school he went to work for the Metropolitan Police at New Scotland Yard for eleven years before discovering the satisfaction of video production. In 1999 he graduated in Broadcast Technical Operations from Ravensbourne College of Design & Communication and was immediately headhunted by QVC UK where he continues to work, currently as a camera supervisor. In his spare time, the author enjoys playing bass guitar semi-professionally, listening to music (mainly of the rock/blues genre!) and following Wasps RFC and the NFL's San Francisco 49ers. He lives in Sussex with his wife, Shirley, has three stepchildren and a granddaughter, Darcy Rose.

A LONDON APPRENTICE — SIR SYDNEY HEDLEY WATERLOW BT.

Chris Waterlow

A LONDON APPRENTICE — SIR
SYDNEY HEDLEY WATERLOW BT.

Vanguard Press

VANGUARD PAPERBACK

© Copyright 2021
Chris Waterlow

The right of Chris Waterlow to be identified as author of
this work has been asserted by him in accordance with the
Copyright, Designs and Patents Act 1988.

A CIP catalogue record for this title is
available from the British Library.

ISBN 978-1-80016-106-1

Vanguard Press is an imprint of
Pegasus Elliot MacKenzie Publishers Ltd.
www.pegasuspublishers.com

First Published in 2021

Vanguard Press
Sheraton House Castle Park
Cambridge England

Printed & Bound in Great Britain

Dedication

This book is dedicated to my wife, Shirley, with thanks for her tolerance, love and understanding.

Acknowledgements

The author would also like to acknowledge and express his gratitude to the following people whose staggering generosity made this publication possible:

Roger & Ruth Shepley

Victoria Ford

Richard Chapple

Peggy McAteer

Peter & Phoebe Noyes

Sophie & Rose

John Waterlow

James & Theresa Waterlow

Samantha Ford Collins

Alexis B Ford Kernot

Chas Watkins

Kathy Olley

Simon Biagi

The Friends of Waterlow Park

There are others who do not wish to be named, but you and I know who you are!

Contents

PREFACE

For as long as I can remember I was brought up with the name of Sydney Hedley Waterlow ringing in my ears. Throughout my childhood the house was always full of reminders and examples of his life and works. When I was three years of age, I was taken by my father to visit Waterlow Park for the first time and to be photographed with the statue of this apparently almost godlike man atop its lofty pedestal looking out over the park and towards the City of London.

Along with the all-too-brief family history lessons, I was also expected to read the official biography of Sydney which, until now, had been the only one written. American author George Smalley had presented this to the world in 1909, three years after Sydney's death, and while the book contains some very useful facts and figures, the style of writing is very much of its time and consequently quite difficult to digest to be of any serious value. Despite this, the book has proved a very useful resource for me as it contains quotations from Sydney himself which were sourced from his private journal, as well as interviews that Smalley undertook during his time spent with his subject. Assuming these are verbatim quotes it also helps to give a rare insight into the mind of this most enigmatic of men and I have absolutely no qualms about including them throughout this version of Sydney's life, and, indeed, it would have possibly been churlish not to do so.

The opening paragraph of Smalley's book recounts how Sydney had wanted his life story to be entitled *The Life of a London Apprentice*; however, it appears that this was not to the liking of the original publishers, thinking that it would only serve to highlight one minor aspect of his outstanding achievements, and so simply decided to re-name it *The Life of Sir Sydney Waterlow, Bart*. As you will have seen, I have all but fulfilled the old man's wishes this time round.

My first genuine interest in my great-great-great grandfather was ignited by a member of the colonial contingent of the Waterlow family, Robert Davis Ford. His grandmother, Hilda, was one of Sydney's children; she had married a naturalised American and they had produced six sons which obviously increased the spread of our family tree substantially. I was eighteen years of age when I first visited Bob and his family in California and it was he who began to indoctrinate me with the appreciation of my family connections and, in particular, Sydney Hedley Waterlow, his great grandfather. Anyone who had ever visited Bob's home at the top of the hill in Ross, California would not have failed to notice the life-size portraits of Sydney and his second wife, Margaret, these having been hung in such a place as to be immediately visible to all on entering the house. Throughout his life, Bob made sure that his children, grandchildren and wider-reaching family were made acutely aware of their heritage. I, for one, will always be eternally grateful that he did so!

Jump forward in time almost forty years and I found myself taking inspiration from Bob's tutelage and enthusiasm to give presentations to some young London schoolchildren about Sydney and the wider Waterlow family as a prelude to Waterlow Park's one hundred and twenty-fifth anniversary celebrations. The preparations for these various events served to re-kindle my desire to promote Sydney and his considerable philanthropic works to a much wider audience.

The names of Charles Dickens and Florence Nightingale are well known for their highlighting of, and contributions to, the improvement of conditions for the countless numbers of the less fortunate in the nineteenth century. However, I am certain that they would have also acknowledged the work of many others, Sydney included, who, for whatever reason, did not remain in the public's collective consciousness.

Sydney was very much a part of this largely unsung group of Victorian men and women such as the likes of journalist and writer Henry Mayhew and wealthy heiress Angela Burdett-Coutts, both of whom worked tirelessly in their own fields of expertise to better the lot of the poor and working classes of that time and with whom Sydney was in regular contact. Despite his many attempts at self-deprecation, Sydney was destined to join the ranks of those remarkable, deserving citizens that most people have never heard of. It is my earnest wish that by the end of this book you will have a better understanding and appreciation of why Sydney Hedley Waterlow undeniably deserves to be included in the group of history's notable and memorable Victorians.

CHAPTER I
EARLY LIFE

Sydney Hedley Waterlow was born the fourth child of seven to James Waterlow and Mary Crakell at their house in Crown Street, Finsbury, London on 1 November 1822. James was a descendant of Walloon Huguenot silk weaving immigrants who had moved over to England during the early part of the seventeenth century having been persecuted out of France by Henry IV.

The origins of the name Waterlow are not entirely clear and there have been many suggestions as to its etymology, some of them not entirely complimentary! The most plausible theory relates to the part of north-eastern France from where the Flemish silk weavers originated. The main area for this industry was centred around Lille, Valenciennes and other small towns; one of these is a community close to Roubaix called Wattrelos, and it is from here that Sydney's forebears appear to have emanated. Walran Waterlow emigrated from this area to Canterbury in 1628 along with other members of his family and friends, all more than likely also involved in the silk weaving trade. Sydney's great-great-great grandfather, Samuel, was born in

Canterbury in 1663 and it was he who eventually moved up to London, no doubt to join other relatives and friends who were looking to make better lives for themselves in the ever-expanding city.

At the age of fourteen, Sydney's father, James, the son of a milk dealer from Mile End, had been bound apprentice to William Witherby at the Stationers' Hall in the City of London on 3 July 1804 and, as was the custom, spent the next seven years learning the trade of a stationer. His first business venture was in 1812 when he became a partner in the firm of Evans & Waterlow, Law Stationers, which had its premises at 1 Freeman's Court, Cornhill and it is quite probable that his wife Mary's wedding dowry helped to fund this enterprise.

James married Mary Crakell on 17 October 1812; sadly, little is known about her. She was born to William and Mary Crakell in London on 12 June 1792, and it is understood she was a tall, beautiful woman with 'dark hair and large black eyes'. She appears to have been a devoted wife and mother, dedicated to the duties of the household including the 'indoor apprentices' who, due to convention, would be boarded and lodged by the master to whom they were indentured. The same had been done for James himself and he was duty bound to follow the traditions and working practices of the well-established system.

On 7 December 1813 James was admitted to Freedom of the Stationers' Company and so was able to begin his amazing rise to fortune and fame and the foundation of a business which was to become the envy of the printing world. However, it is Sydney himself who can best describe his own early life:

'I was born before I was expected, and was altogether such a tiny, miserable piece of humanity that my father said he could have put me into a quart-pot and laid his hand on top of it without any difficulty. There were no clothes ready for me; nobody thought I should live, and I was kept in a blanket for a fortnight. But by degrees my father and mother began to think that, if there was not much in the flesh, there was a good deal in the spirit, and that perhaps they might save me. So they made me some clothes, but I was so sick and ailing that, when I was about two months old, my mother sent me to my grandmother Waterlow at Mile End, where I lived till I was six years old.

'At that time Mile End was a pleasant country road, bright and sunny. I can recollect spending many an hour sitting on the doorstep, under a rustic wooden porch, watching the hay-carts going to the Whitechapel market; and the four-horse coaches which ran to London, passing to or from the north and east of London. I was still, however, a small weakling, for my aunt Mary, who lived with her mother, often told me that she used to take me out of bed in the morning, turn me over in her left hand, and with her right pump water on my weak little back in order to strengthen the spine.'

As well as this very traumatic start to life, Sydney's general childhood was not to improve with any great significance, being one of suffering and of dreary and cruel experiences. He twice narrowly escaped death; once being swept into the local canal and having to be hauled out of the water by the bargemen, and once straying into a sugar refinery, "full of immense coppers of boiling sugar", and being shut in there. Luckily, he was aware of the risk of stumbling about among the vast caldrons and so wisely sat down and screamed until workmen came to rescue him — he was four years of age.

His first taste of education was at a school in Worship Street run by two sisters named Bone. There he was taught to read and write and the meaning of school discipline. It was the custom for these ladies to rope together any rebellious pupils and to leave them standing bound together for several hours at a time; this treatment was combined with the use of more familiar forms of punishment. Two years later, at the age of seven, Sydney was sent away to boarding school in Brighton. The master had been a retail grocer who had become bankrupt and had stumbled into the teaching profession. The man was quite unsuited for the job, being harsh and cruel, and Sydney finally left in 1831 having suffered much and learning little.

The next establishment was to be much closer to home, St Saviour's Grammar School, Southwark; situated at the southern end of the old London Bridge, this was three miles from his parents' new house in Gloucester Terrace, Hoxton. In those days this was on the very edge of the ever-expanding London with market gardens and fields facing the property. Sydney would have to rise early, breakfast at six o'clock and be in school by eight, having to make the three-mile journey painfully on foot. At that time there were few cabs, no omnibuses and, of course, no railways.

'I distinctly remember seeing the first omnibus that ever started in London. It was built by a man named Shillibeer, who carried on a large business as undertaker. It was painted bright blue, and ran from Paddington to Bank, and a shilling fare was charged in competition with the eighteen-penny fare of the stagecoach. It is difficult in these days to imagine London without omnibuses, but I am not sure whether, when people walked more, they were not healthier.'

It is very possible that his elder brothers might have walked with him as Birchin Lane, the site of the family business, was a short distance from the bridge, and no doubt Sydney might have wished he was going to work with them, or anywhere other than school.

The master of St Saviour's was the Reverend Lancelot Sharpe, a canon of St Paul's Cathedral and a 'splendid classical scholar'. However, it appears he was not quite the avuncular character one would imagine him to be. One stormy winter's morning Sydney had the misfortune to arrive some fifteen minutes late; when asked the reason for his tardiness he explained that he had sought shelter from the worst of the storm in a shop doorway and was promptly knocked to the ground by

Sharpe who remarked, "There! The next time it rains tie hay-bands around your legs and come through it!" The canon was very much a believer in the maxim 'spare the rod, spoil the child', and if he considered Sydney's academic progress to be falling behind, would beat the boy until his back was covered with blood.

'But as a young boy, I am afraid I was rather obstinate, wilful and difficult to control, with a keen sense of any injustice.

'The curriculum of St Saviour's School was most incomplete. Beyond writing and arithmetic, and Latin, Greek, and Hebrew, no subjects of any kind were taught. The boys had no opportunity of learning anything about English grammar, composition, history, geography. This was a severe loss to me, and one whose effects were felt all through life; for during the whole of my apprenticeship I never had any time whatever for reading or study, and it was not until after I was twenty-one years of age that I was able to devote any time to these things, and even then, only a few hours could be taken occasionally, as all my efforts were devoted to the establishment, and development of my business.'

After escaping comparatively lightly from a severe blow delivered by a pump handle to the frontal bone of his eye which nearly lost him his sight and left a permanent mark, Sydney embarked, while still at St Saviour's, on a new adventure and one which has now vanished for ever:

'Whenever we boys could raise a shilling amongst us, our great delight was to hire a wherry at Bankside and to row on the river, shooting one of the narrow arches of old London Bridge. At that time this was a dangerous feat, for the arches were so narrow, and caused such an obstruction to the ebb and flow of the tide, that there was a fall of two or three feet on every arch, excepting the two large arches in the middle of the river. This old bridge, with its picturesque quaintness, still remains a vivid picture in my memory, as I used to cross it twice a day during the first two or three years of my London school life. Those who never saw it would scarcely realise that the roadway of the bridge was no higher than the road was at Lower Thames Street, which now passes under the land arch of the present London Bridge.'

However, Sydney summarises his school life in practical terms:

'Soon after I was eleven years old, I commenced learning Greek, and I had to begin Hebrew before I was thirteen. During the whole four and a half years that I attended St Saviour's School nearly all my time was devoted to the three dead languages — Latin, Greek and Hebrew. Sometimes I wished that they were not only dead, but decently buried, beyond all hope of resurrection.

'Most men are able to look back on their school days as a period of pleasure and happiness, full of recollections of holidays spent in the enjoyment of games and sports of all kinds; but my school days were an unhappy exception to this rule. My life, from the time I first went to an infant school to the period when I began my apprenticeship, was hard and cheerless. The customary holidays, and even the half-holidays, of school life were spent in assisting in my father's business; and with the exception of some mid-summer holidays which I once enjoyed at Gravesend — then regarded as a seaside resort — I am able to recall but few pleasant or happy periods in my early life.

'It is, of course, difficult to say whether this rough early training was not a better preparation for the strenuous labours of my seven years' apprenticeship, and the subsequent struggles on my own account, than a careless, easy-going experience in these youthful days would have been. At the same time, this early contact with all those who had to depend on their own exertions for their daily bread doubtless increased and developed my sympathy and interest in the working classes.'

While Sydney may have respected the headmaster of St Saviour's, he certainly held no affection for him. However, there was one man whom he acknowledged as having a profound influence on him. This was the well-known Unitarian minister William Johnson Fox (1786–1864), a preacher, politician and man of letters. James Waterlow had been baptised into the Church of England as were all his children although it appears that at some stage, after 1829, he joined the congregation at Fox's chapel in South Place, Finsbury. It was here, sitting in the family pew, that Sydney became inspired by Fox, something which was to manifest itself later in his many philanthropic activities:

'A complete copy of Mr Fox's works is still regarded by me as one of the most valuable portions of my library. I never think of him without feeling that I owe more to him, perhaps, than to any other man outside of my own family.'

CHAPTER II
A LONDON APPRENTICE

Sydney's formal education came to an abrupt halt on 1 November 1836, his fourteenth birthday, when he accompanied his father to Stationers' Hall to attend the traditional ceremony of being bound apprentice, just as his father had done over thirty years earlier. He was to be apprenticed to Thomas Harrison, his uncle, for a period of seven years, during which time he would learn in detail about the printing trade in its entirety. This meant that once he had obtained his Freedom, he would be able to start out in business on his own as being fully qualified in the trade.

Thomas Harrison was a master printer with a large business in Orchard Street, Westminster being private printer to the Government Press at the Foreign Office. For the next seven years Sydney lived as a member of his uncle's family, first in Coleshill Street, Pimlico then in Westbourne Terrace at the north-east corner of Sloane Square. His uncle and aunt had five small children, with two more arriving before Sydney had left in 1843, so he was not entirely deprived of adolescent company. Thomas Harrison was the kind of master who could be described as 'firm but fair'; he showed no favouritism towards his young nephew and ensured that he received a thorough training in his work. Despite having to work long, hard days, Sydney would always look back on his apprenticeship as a time of happiness and would never complain about the severity of the task in hand. He recalls walking with his uncle to start his first day's work in Orchard Street, near Westminster Abbey:

'He took me by the hand, I remember, down to his office, and I walked home with him in the evening, for I lived with him as member of his own family and received personal instruction and attention. It is much to be regretted that this system does not obtain at present. My sons take apprentices every year, but they do not live with them as I did with my master, but their parents provide them with a sufficient sum of money to live near the business.'

When Sydney began his apprenticeship, the traditional 'indoor' system had already begun to break down as far as the larger printing firms were concerned; in fact, most master printers' wives would have reeled in horror at the thought of having to provide food and lodging for twenty or more boisterous teenagers.

Now that Sydney had been shown once how to find the premises in Orchard Street, he was then expected to make his own way to and from work:

'I used to walk every day from my master's house near Sloane Square to Orchard Street, Westminster, then one of the vilest dens in the whole of London.

Close by was a quadrangle known as the Almonry, reached by two arches, one at either end. It was the property of the ecclesiastical authorities situated by the monastery. To describe the squalor, misery and crime that was then concentrated in this square patch is almost impossible. Thieves, pickpockets, men and women of the lowest type herded there, and you will gather some ideas of its terrible condition when I tell you that only the boldest of us dare to go through it even in broad daylight.'

So not only was this place inhabited by a substantial portion of the criminal population of London, it was also home to a vast assortment of very unpleasant illnesses. Consequently, because Sydney was so young and was being exposed to these contagions on a daily basis, within a year of working in the area he was struck down with 'black typhus' (now known as Bolivian haemorrhagic fever) which is transmitted through airborne particles of rodent urine which must have been prevalent given the general poor sanitation of the area. In those days it was not unknown for the sufferer to be dead within twenty-four hours. However, Sydney fought it for three months, the entire Harrison household fleeing the building with the exception of one old woman servant who nursed him through it. This experience must have developed an iron constitution within the lad as he lived free from illness of any kind for the next twenty-three years.

The first two years of Sydney's apprenticeship was taken up with learning about the work of the compositor including how to set type, and although situated in such an undesirable area, the printing office was in an ideal place to service some of its most important customers such as the Foreign Office. The firm had also been printing *The London Gazette* for the past seventy-five years, and so Sydney's training was taking place in a good, well-established business and not some small, pokey backstreet firm.

Not long after Sydney had mastered all the components of composition, Harrison was commissioned to print a history of British India which contained a large number of quotations in Arabic, Hebrew, Coptic, Syriac and other Middle Eastern languages. As Sydney had studied Hebrew under the Reverend Sharpe at St Saviour's, his uncle gave him the responsibility of setting all the foreign texts. So, with the help of Mr Morris, Secretary of the Royal Asiatic Society, he managed to set up, not only the Hebrew, but all the other texts in all the other languages. Of course, Harrison was no fool: he knew full well that he was getting a long, arduous job done for nothing, as Sydney would not be receiving any wages as an apprentice. It must also not be forgotten that the terms of the apprenticeship meant that he had to work without payment for fifty weeks of the year for seven years:

'I was allowed a fortnight's holiday once a year, in the autumn. I remember that, when the time for the second annual holiday arrived, I told my master there was a certain irony in taking a holiday when I had no money, and I reminded him that I had worked a good many extra hours during the previous eighteen months. But he seemed deaf or did not want to understand that I would like some holiday allowance. When he had left the room, I appealed to my mistress, who was a very kind-hearted woman. She said she would see what could be done, and the next day my master gave me three pounds, to my delight. This was the first money I ever earned, but I had acquired such a mastery of my trade by that time as to be able to do work that could be measured and paid for as piecework. On returning from my holidays, my master said I must not rely upon a precedent having been established for my next holiday, and that I must earn money for myself. I acquiesced in his proposal and took the opportunity of requesting him to put me upon piecework, and he consented to do so if we could agree upon the terms. It was at length arranged that for two years I was to earn eighteen shillings a week for him, and to have for myself a third of anything I could earn beyond that sum. For the ensuing three years I was to earn twenty-two shillings a week for him, and to have half of all I earned beyond that. This arrangement not only stimulated me to work as hard as I could during regular hours, but eagerly to secure all the overwork I could possibly obtain.'

In order to get a rough idea of what Sydney would have to have done in order to earn his 18/- per week, reference can be made to *The London Scale of Prices for Compositors' Work*, published by the London Union of Compositors in 1836. It was usual to work a twelve-hour day for six days a week, although on Saturdays some offices allowed their staff to go home in the late afternoon as a concession. Sydney would have been paid an average of 6d per 1,000 ens (letters), and so to earn 18/- he would have had to have set about 34,000 ens, which would have taken him about four hours. In the remaining time he could have set another 26,000 ens, which would have earned him another 5/-. On the assumption that he could average 1,250 ens per hour during the last three years of his apprenticeship, it is quite likely that his average weekly earnings were 11/- on top of the original 22/- earned for completing the quota. (At this time skilled compositors were earning between 36/- and 40/- per week.) After four years of apprenticeship, at the age of eighteen, Sydney's undoubted skill as a printer led Harrison to put him in charge of the composing section for Foreign Office and Cabinet jobs, and owing to the confidential nature of the work the equipment was actually housed in Downing Street itself:

'Before I was eighteen, Mr Harrison gave me work in connection with the private press at Downing Street. I afterwards entirely superintended this press. I can recollect still the awful labour it was to drag the formes [*iron frames containing the pages of type*] up those

31

narrow old-fashioned stairs to the third floor back in Downing Street.'

He had to receive and oversee the implementation of orders, hire extra staff, make out the weekly pay sheets and pay the men; good business training for the future. He also received no extra money for this work but took his share of the more profitable piecework jobs.

So, it was with this regular income starting to appear that Sydney began to save, opening an account at the St Martin's Lane Savings Bank. By the time he had obtained his Freedom he managed to accrue thirty pounds in this account which afforded him the opportunity of independence. His average earning for each of the seven years of his apprenticeship was very nearly £4 5s 10d per year. From the age of sixteen he had cost his father nothing with the exception of a clothing allowance. Pocket money, holiday expenses and all other overheads, except the board and lodging provided by his master, he had provided for himself.

'No thirty pounds, nor many times thirty pounds, ever gave me so much pleasure as these savings, nor were of so much use.'

During his time at the Foreign Office, Sydney was able to build up a good working relationship with several members of the staff. Edmund Hammond (later to become Baron Hammond of Kirkella), who had been the permanent under-secretary for over twenty years, was especially kind to the lad, and the friendly relations between them lasted until Hammond's death in 1890.

There was a Mr Mellish, a senior clerk of whom it is recorded that, although violent in temper, he was never unjust. All the heads of departments treated the master apprentice with consideration, having discovered that he was clearly of exceptional talent. About a certain Mr Cunningham, another of the senior clerks, Sydney is recorded as saying:

'He was a tall, heavy man with a wooden leg — a great advantage to us printers, as we could always hear him as he stumped along the passage leading to our rooms. One day he had sent work back for alterations, and, not receiving it as soon as he expected, he came into the printing offices and expostulated with me. I was in the act of correcting the type as fast as I could and tried to explain the difficulties we had to contend with. My hair was very long and fell over my eyes. He exclaimed: "Hold your tongue, sir, and get your hair cut." He seemed to fancy that the length of my hair interfered with rapidity and efficiency of the work.'

There were, however, occasional moments of relaxation:

'The work at the Foreign Office was very fitful. On some days we had scarcely anything to do; then came a sudden rush to get private documents printed for a Cabinet meeting, the pressure upon the small number of hands often compelling me to work all night, and sometimes on Sundays. I remember one Saturday, in the middle of summer, we had had no work for one or two days, so at twelve o'clock we made up a party for a row on the river, taking a four-oared boat from Searle's boat house at Westminster Bridge. I rowed an oar in the bows to Kew and back, reaching the Foreign Office again about five p.m., when I found, to my horror, that I had been sent for several times. Some important work had to be done for a Cabinet meeting at three o'clock on Sunday.

'In those days Sunday was the favourite day for Cabinet meetings. Our number of hands was small, and, being Saturday afternoon, it was difficult to get any assistance; so, after our vigorous exercise on the river, we had to work all night — in fact, we did not get finished until midday on Sunday.

'Documents of a most confidential character were constantly placed in my hands to be printed. Before the passing of the Bank Charter Act of 1844 private banks throughout England and Wales had the privilege of issuing notes to an unlimited amount, provided that the public in the locality were willing to accept them. As a natural consequence, a run upon the banks was not an infrequent occurrence, and these runs often led to riots, with serious disturbance to the public peace and loss to those who held the notes. In 1843 Sir Robert Peel's government came to the conclusion that fresh legislation was imperatively necessary, and therefore called for a return from each of the banks issuing notes, which was to be supplied in the form of an ordinary debtor and creditor balance-sheet, showing the number of notes in circulation, and the assets and liabilities of each bank issuing them. These balance-sheets and the statements accompanying them the government undertook to keep strictly private and confidential. Having charge of these documents during the time they were being printed, I had to use the greatest care to see that none of the information contained in them leaked out, and that no copy of them was surreptitiously conveyed out of the office. The passing of the Bank Charter Act in the following year remedied the existing evil, as from that time none of the banks were permitted to issue a larger number of notes than that which was in circulation at the date when the bill received the Royal Assent. Since that period the circulation of notes issued by private banks has been considerably reduced, and Bank of England notes substituted.'

So, Sydney remained in this great position of trust and responsibility until the expiration of his indentures in 1843. During the seven years of his apprenticeship, it is quite evident that he had learned a good deal more than the skill and art of printing. He had been introduced to and successfully managed both administrative and executive duties and had to deal with both the workforce and business accounting. He had become a wheel in the great machine of government and had established a connection with one or more of the permanent officials on whom the smooth running of any government relies.

It appears that Sydney had formed such a good working relationship with his uncle that it was his hope and, possibly, also his expectation to continue the partnership after being granted his Freedom. Sadly, however, Harrison was not in a position to offer him any permanent work and so Sydney had to find something which would put his hard-earned skills to good use. As the final two weeks of his indentures coincided with his last holiday he was allowed to leave early, and at the end of October 1843 went home to visit his parents.

As Sydney had been trained as a letterpress printer, there was not even a position available to him at the Waterlow firm in Birchin Lane. By this stage this consisted of the stationery side of the business and the small lithographic section which was then managed by his eldest brother, Alfred. So, rather than looking for a job in London, he decided to take himself off to Paris with the intention of learning to speak French and to find work as a compositor. It is not clear whether his father, James, gave him any money to help him on his way, but the money he had managed to save from the extra piecework he had done for Harrison over the previous years provided a good, sound financial grounding to help him get started.

Sydney only had one contact in Paris: a friend who was employed as clerk in a large drapery shop in the Rue Castiglione. He was also able to rent a fireless room in the same house where his friend lodged in the Rue St Niçaise, opposite the Palais Royal, for thirty francs a month. However, after trudging round the streets of Paris for two weeks looking for work and finding none, he had almost resigned himself to accepting a job, as a shop assistant, in the same store as his friend, for the princely sum of one franc per day. Luckily, he gained a last-minute reprieve when he was taken on as a compositor by Monsieur Galignani, a publisher, bookseller and newspaper owner, who invited Sydney to print a catalogue of his library for twenty francs a week which was the regular printer's wages in Paris at that time. Although the job was welcome, the conditions in which he had to work were far from ideal. He had to labour all winter long in a freezing room with a tiled floor and no fire. However, grateful for the job, Sydney continued, and his father, on getting news that his son was following his trade, sent him ten pounds as a sign of approval and encouragement; so, Sydney continued until the spring of 1844 when the catalogue was finally finished.

During this time, he had gone to live with a French professor in the Avenue Châteaubriand, high up in the Champs Elysées quarter. The professor was married to an English woman, and he had agreed to taking in Sydney and to teach him French and German for a small weekly payment. The professor and his wife were a generous couple and more than happy to help the young man whose intention was to eventually travel to Frankfurt or Leipzig which were considered great centres for book publishing and where there would always be jobs for good, qualified compositors. However, the German adventure never materialised, as, following earnest discussions back in London, Sydney received a letter from his brother, Alfred, on the direct request from their father.

In essence, the letter set out a proposal; in the past it had not been thought possible that the profits from the law stationery business would be sufficient to support all five sons. This had been the reason why brother Charles had entered the building trade and Sydney had been apprenticed to a letterpress printer. It appeared as if the family had now reached the conclusion that Sydney's undoubted expertise in letterpress would be beneficial to both the firm and to Sydney himself. As a result, it had been decided that the business would be equipped with a small letterpress department of which Sydney would be offered the management at a starting salary of three pounds per week (if he would care to accept the post!). In addition, Sydney would be invited to join in partnership with his father and brothers, Alfred and Walter, provided that father, James, was guaranteed an income equal to the average profits for the last three years and to divide the remainder equally between them.

Sydney did not need to be asked twice and returned to London immediately. He was already at work by Easter 1844 at additional premises leased in London Wall. From that moment on the pace and expansion of the family firm was to be fast and furious.

CHAPTER III
WATERLOW & SONS

On his return to England, Sydney was quick to discover that the promised partnership was only dependent on the creation of an additional business to supplement the current operation being run by his father and elder brothers. In order to accommodate Sydney's section of the firm a whole new department was going to have to be established. The current enterprise, as founded by James, was predominantly dealing with law stationery, general stationery and the manufacture of account books.

Sydney himself had had no say in the new scheme which had been solely devised by his father and brothers. It had been his brother Alfred who had written to him in Paris, and it was also Alfred, together with Walter, who had persuaded their father to expand the business in this new direction. Alfred's expansion argument to his father was that James still had a large family which was almost totally dependent on him for income and that he could only afford to allow his sons a share in the profits if the business and its profits could be increased. It was therefore agreed that this could best be done by the addition of a printing concern to

39

supplement the existing stationery business. Sydney was attracted to the proposition on two counts; the first being that he was able to join the growing family business and, secondly, that he was allowed to set up the printing section from scratch and to his own satisfaction.

The financial arrangement was not exactly overwhelming, but Sydney was to be paid, initially, the sum of three pounds per week which would be augmented according to the success of the enterprise. This was not an impressive sum by any means, but it was more than three times the amount he had been earning working on the composition of Monsieur Galignani's catalogue huddled up in a fireless room throughout a Paris winter. Sydney was also acutely aware that although commercial printing was still in its infancy, he recognised its undoubted potential and was keen to exploit "the potentiality of growing rich beyond the dreams of avarice".

So, in Easter week 1844, Sydney, not yet twenty-two years of age, returned to England to take up his challenge. In order to get the ball rolling, a modest outlay of one hundred and twenty pounds was made to stock the small printing office with type, two second-hand iron presses and a small wooden Caxton press. With a man and boy to help him, he began printing in March of that year, producing the *Banker's Magazine*, with the first edition appearing in April. The publication was edited by a Mr J. S. Dalton, a clerk in the

Provisional Bank of Ireland in Broad Street, with the profits from sales being divided between the editor and printers in fixed proportion.

It was not long before the proposed partnership followed. James Waterlow was now satisfied that the lithographic and general printing returns, in addition to the stationery and account book profits, warranted this step. James' four sons, Alfred, Walter, Sydney and Albert, who up until then, were no more than employees of the business, were all included in the partnership deed. James was happy to hand over a substantial amount of the workload to his sons who were now to give their whole time to the business and would be jointly and severally liable to the whole capital. In return, James was to receive an annual sum roughly equivalent to the total of the three years' average annual profits before the partnership began. The sons were to equally divide what remained, and none of the partners was to hold shares in any bank or other joint-stock enterprise in which there was a liability on the shares.

As luck would have it, the formation of this partnership in 1844 happened to coincide with the meteoric development of the railway system in Great Britain. The new firm of Messrs Waterlow & Sons were fortunate enough early on to acquire a good share of the large printing and stationery business of the new transportation marvel. At the time, the company had less than twenty employees on a weekly wage, but there was to be a steady and rapid increase in the workload and a pressing need for an expansion of business premises. A lease was taken from the Carpenters' Company for their buildings at 66-67 London Wall, and this was to be the first of many transactions with that company. The houses were in front of Carpenters' Hall itself, with the main entrance forming part of 68 London Wall. James Waterlow, being the cautious man that he was, insisted that only the ground floor of the premises be used by the firm, the other three floors being let to provide additional income. Such was the pace of the expansion of the firm that it soon became necessary to take back use of the whole building.

The reasons for this unprecedented escalation in fortunes were several. In 1843, the firm was principally involved in law and manufacturing stationery and could offer an additional lithographic printing service. This small department had been in existence for about ten years but there is no reason to believe that it was anything other than a complementary side-line. There is little doubt, however, that the contacts made in connection with this department played no small part in finding work for the letterpress department when it began to operate under Sydney's management in 1844. This then had a knock-on effect, as the speedy and successful development of the letterpress department meant that other parts of the business could now also be expanded.

The fifteen or so weekly-wage earners in the employment of Waterlow & Sons in 1844 had grown to over four thousand by 1898. The company by then had ten establishments in the City of London, one in Westminster and one at Dunstable. The London Wall premises were retained and utilised as a retail department for general stationery, account books, envelopes and stamps. The registered offices were in Great Winchester Street where there was shipping departments, general offices for the receipt of orders and other correspondence, general warehouses, the law form and agency department, banknote and commercial engraving, copperplate printing, law and surveyors' lithography, engrossment of deeds and editorial departments. In the Finsbury stationery works there was commercial and general printing, machine ruling, account book making, lithography, engineering, security-plate printing, the illumination of testimonials and other matters. In other factories there was cardboard making, railway ticket printing and account book binding as well as printing and binding, under contract, between Waterlow's and the government. There were also warehouses for packing and 'baling' of export goods, carpenters' and cabinetmakers' shops for the manufacture of ticket-issue cases and copying-press stands. In the Paul Street works, envelope-making, die-sinking, medal striking and seal engraving. There were the Law and Parliament stationery departments at 49 & 50 Parliament Street, Westminster along with parliamentary and lithographic printing rooms for the production of plans and sections, reference books and all forms necessary for parliamentary deposits.

Waterlow & Sons were also contractors for supplying stationery to the Great Western, Great Northern, South Western and Brighton railways among others. They also had contracts with Indian and Egyptian railways and some of the great steamship companies of the time. They dealt with many large and municipal banking corporations, colonial and many foreign governments. They printed and published the *Banking Almanac*, the *Solicitor's Diary* and the *Solicitor's Pocket Book*, the *Banker's Magazine* as well as many books on law. They printed money for home, colonial and foreign governments; they supplied postage stamps and postcards to foreign countries. The name of Waterlow became a certificate of quality.

Throughout this time of growth, it was Sydney's earnest wish that the company employees were to share in the good fortunes of the firm and to benefit from financial recognition for their work above and beyond the regular wages they already received. So, the company created a bonus scheme whereby all its salaried staff were each to receive a Christmas bonus; this was calculated as a percentage of their salaries equal to the percentage paid to the company's shareholders as a dividend. If the shareholders got a five per cent dividend, the employees received five per cent of their salaries as a bonus. This worked so well, that the scheme was extended beyond the salaried staff to everyone in the firm. The employees were also divided into two groups; overseers and sub-foremen, and workmen/women. Four funds were created: death assurance; retiring allowance; sick fund augmentation and emergency cases. In addition to these, the firm endeavoured to ensure that the workforce was looked after on a day-to-day basis and this had the effect of making the employees feel like valued members of the organisation which, naturally, in turn led to greater productivity.

The fact that the business was operating on such a vast scale is proof that this was due to the hard work of many people, but what was also evident was that the driving force for many years was, in fact, Sydney himself. He had laid the basic foundations for progress and had designed a large part of the superstructure of the business model; he clearly had a large amount of creative energy. Without his input, Waterlow & Sons would have become a very different animal with a completely different story to tell. He had impressed his personality upon the firm; the liberal policy towards the employees including the thought and care for their comfort, health and general well-being was predominantly his idea. It is also true to say that all this would not have been achievable on his own; he was astute enough to gather people around him who were to become like family to him in ensuring the success of the great venture. Great credit was also due to his father, James, who had the foresight to trust in his sons, Sydney in particular. Credit also to the brothers, Alfred, Walter and Albert who devoted their time and energies to the various other branches of the business. However, because of his time spent as an apprentice working with his uncle, Sydney had a very detailed knowledge of the printing business, and printing was, and continued to be, the source and chief provider of the company's fortunes for well over another hundred years. With a dozen establishments based in the City of London, Westminster and Dunstable, there were many tributes to his endeavours. However, as we shall see, there were and are far more recognisable monuments for which he should and would have preferred to be remembered, but none of these would have existed without the former.

Long before the family business had had time to grow into a great dynasty, Sydney was more than satisfied that he had sown the seeds for success and felt reassured that it would continue to grow and prosper accordingly. He was never a man to rest on his laurels, and within a year of joining the firm he had made up his mind to marry. After a brief engagement, he married Anna Maria Hickson, the daughter of a London merchant and manufacturer who had a country home, Fairseat, in Wrotham, Kent. Sydney had known Anna Maria for some time but had decided that he would not be in a position to ask for her hand in marriage until her family, especially her father, thought him to be an eligible suitor. It is almost certain that their acquaintance dated from his time as an apprentice, as

Sydney was not even twenty-three years of age when the marriage took place on 7 May 1845. They lived together very happily, with Anna Maria bearing Sydney twelve children. She died in Nice on 21 January 1880, sadly preceded by the death of their eldest son, John, in Genoa, on 4 December 1871. Anna Maria was a gentle, affectionate, delicate woman by all accounts, devoted to her husband and her children and loved by all who knew her.

CHAPTER IV
ENTRANCE INTO PUBLIC LIFE

In the years following his marriage to Anna Maria, Sydney became immersed in business and family life. The success of the family firm, and of Sydney in particular, naturally brought him to the attention of the civil business community of the City of London. In 1857 the resignation of a common councilman in the Broad Street ward in the City created a vacancy and Sydney was asked to stand for selection. He was duly elected without opposition and so began his life in public service. In typical style, Sydney made it his priority to master this new 'trade'. He spent a year learning how municipal business was conducted in committees and in the Court of Common Council. He then began to take an active part in the proceedings, starting with the police force.

At that time there was almost nothing in the way of general public or private electrical communication except what had been installed along the main lines of the railway system. It occurred to Sydney that the overall efficiency of the City of London Police would be greatly enhanced if the commissioner's office and his residence in Finsbury Circus were to be connected by telegraph with all the City's police stations. There was one major snag: there were no overhead wires in the City. So, Sydney's first job was to try and persuade his partners in Waterlow's to allow him to establish a telegraphic service between the firm's factory in London Wall and their business house in Parliament Street, Westminster. His brothers readily agreed to the plan, trusting Sydney's foresight of the project; and so, with the help of a builder by the name of Matthew Allen, and a Mr Rowland, a clerk to a firm of solicitors in Copthall Court, he began construction of the telegraph line. This was quite an undertaking for all of them as none had any knowledge of electrical engineering!

Any physical difficulties were met and dealt with as they arose. Allen invented a cast-iron saddle to straddle the ridgepoles of the houses and to receive the masts for the wires. Such was the suitability of these saddles that they appear to have been widely adopted for similar installations by other companies for some time afterwards. As the roofs of the houses were completely untouched by the wires or by other parts of the equipment, the owners of the houses offered no objections to the solution. There was one dissenter however, the Drapers' Company; although no wire was due to be fixed to any part of their hall, an objection was raised that it was not possible for the wire to even pass over the roof of the building. The company insisted that they owned the freehold of the land from the centre of the earth to the "canopy of Heaven".

Finally, after some skilful negotiation, terms were settled; Waterlow & Sons agreed to pay the Drapers' Company the sum of half a crown per year for the right to stretch a wire through the air of Heaven — or rather Heaven and the Drapers' Company! From there the line then ran to the Waterlow's premises in Birchin Lane, on to Southwark Bridge and across the Thames to the south side of the river. Then, passing along the taller of the buildings, it travelled up to Hungerford Bridge, crossing back over the river again and on up to Parliament Street. Sydney recalled:

'This last was a long stretch, and we could not prevent the wire from sagging. When first placed in position, it came so low that sailing barges frequently raised their topmasts with the object of pulling it down.'

As this was achieved several times, the wire was eventually replaced with one made of light steel which could be kept taut enough to deter any further attempts by mischievous boat crews. The total expense of the installation, including three sending/receiving instruments of the Charles Wheatstone design, was less than one hundred pounds; ultimately the installation was taken over by the Post Office.

The commissioner of the City Police at this time, until his death in 1863, was one Daniel Whittle Harvey. He had been a very radical politician but, in total contrast, had extremely conservative views regarding police management. He had a strong dislike for Sydney's telegraph scheme and told the police committee that he thought it would be far too easy for the wires to be tapped into so that police secrets would be disclosed, and consequently the committee rejected the whole idea on that basis. However, Sydney did not take 'no' for an answer and refused to give in without a fight. He appeared before the committee again with a new plan whereby the telegraph wires were only to be attached to church belfries to which the general public had no access. This time the suggestion was accepted without any hesitation and Commissioner Harvey offered no resistance to the new scheme. A contract was drawn up with Messrs Henley, a firm of telegraph engineers which allowed for the six City police stations and the commissioner's office to be connected to each other, and the whole job was completed for the princely sum of three hundred pounds.

At the conclusion of the trial, the police committee reported back to the Court of Common Council that the test had been a complete success. The Court whereupon gave a unanimous vote of thanks to Sydney:

'for his persevering exertions in originating and developing the plan for establishing a telegraphic communication between the police stations of the City of London, which has proved by its results, not only highly useful in facilitating the operations of the police force, but also beneficial to the public in cases of emergency and danger.'

This was to be Sydney's first of many official recognitions for his efforts in public service and it appears that he had applied the same principles of action in this as he had found useful in his private business. He had done the job as well and as cheaply as he had been able, and throughout his life he ensured that he employed the same energy and resourcefulness irrespective of any potential profit.

CHAPTER V
ALDERMAN AND SHERIFF

Sydney's service with the Common Council lasted a little over five years, from 1857 until early 1863. In November 1862, Mr Alderman Cubitt, who had twice been lord mayor, announced his retirement as Alderman of Langbourn ward and Sydney was immediately encouraged to offer himself up as a candidate for the vacancy. Sydney's response was typical in that as he did not live in the ward, he did not consider himself eligible; although this was by no means a legal requirement, it was a usual condition of the office. He was, however, reminded that the Birchin Lane premises of Waterlow & Sons was only two or three doors away from the ward boundary line, and so with his friends continuing to press him, he eventually accepted the nomination.

Within a few days of this, half a dozen other candidates had also declared their interest. Out of two hundred electors, sixty pledged their allegiance to Sydney, the first two being Mr H. S. Thornton of Williams Deacon & Co., bankers, and Mr George G. Glyn, head of the Glyn Mills banking house. The contest lasted eleven weeks instead of the more usual two or three and there were many twists and turns to the events. One opponent after another gradually withdrew until only a Mr Andrew Lusk remained. Things then started to get a little personal with Sydney's religious views being called into question: he was a Unitarian; Lusk was a Presbyterian. "Will you vote for an unbeliever?" cried some of Lusk's supporters. Eventually, Andrew Lusk withdrew from the contest and Sydney must have finally thought that the position was all but his. Suddenly from nowhere a Mr Charles Capper, Manager of the London and Victoria Docks, was nominated by railway contractor Sir Samuel Peto, then a well-known industrialist.

The official nomination took place on 29 January 1863 in the Langbourn ward schoolrooms, presided over by the lord mayor, Sir William Rose. As was usual, the voting was done by a show of hands, but Capper decided that this was not going to be conclusive and demanded a proper poll which was duly held the following day. By the end of the day's polling the results were as follows:

Waterlow 126

Capper 74

So began Sydney's long and distinguished service in the Court of Aldermen which was to last for over twenty years — he was forty years of age.

An eminent Lord Chancellor once said to Sydney that he knew of no legal work more important or more onerous than the summary administration of justice, and that, generally, there was no better place where it was carried out than in the City of London. This served to greatly encourage and inspire the new Mr Alderman Waterlow as he began his new duties as a magistrate. He had much to learn in this new role including the more mundane municipal obligations, but, as was his way, the drive to achieve was no less powerful for any of these.

His first duty outside of the usual routine as a magistrate was to visit the mentally ill who were, at that time, under the charge of the Corporation of London. The City of London itself was not responsible for the maintenance of any asylums for these poor unfortunates who lived within the City's boundaries, but the magistrates were responsible for the custody of mentally ill vagrants found within the City limits. In those days it was common practice for other countries to stow their mentally ill citizens aboard ships headed for the Port of London ensuring they were put ashore wherever the ship happened to anchor. This had the result that a large majority of the mentally ill people in the City were from other countries and ended up being cared for by the City in private asylums. Sydney investigated this situation with his usual thoroughness, personally examining the asylums and their guests. In later years he was to become a magistrate for Middlesex and a member of the Committee of the County Asylum at Colney Hatch. He visited the establishment weekly over the period of a year and became convinced that public asylums were far superior in every way to their private equivalents. Along with some of his colleagues, he carried a proposal for the City Asylum at Stone, near Dartford, Kent, which was subsequently built and administered for over a century until it was eventually closed for re-development in 2005.

Four years after his successful election to alderman, Sydney now had to make the far-reaching decision as to whether he should present himself for election to sheriff of London. Then, as now, if you have the drive and ambition to become lord mayor of London you must progress along a time-honoured route, part of which includes service in the office of sheriff. There was now no doubt in Sydney's mind that he wished to become lord mayor; he had identified himself with the City and had the natural and inevitable ambition of a man set on this course. It appears that the City had no objection to his desire, and he was elected to the office of sheriff on 29 September 1866 serving under Lord Mayor Gabriel, a man Sydney liked and greatly respected.

One of the more unsavoury duties incumbent upon the sheriff was having to attend prison, and, in particular, witnessing the discharging of capital punishment sentences, something which repulsed Sydney but he, nevertheless, undertook the task faithfully. Executions at this time were still public affairs, and, fortunately, Sydney only had to attend one of these. He described the scene in his journal to which he added his own reflections on the system itself:

'It is astonishing to think how long these public executions continued in a city claiming to be the most civilised on the face of the earth. No one who has ever witnessed the scene can resist the conclusion that, instead of acting as a deterrent, it actually created a fascination and a craving for notoriety which rather stimulated than diminished the tendency to crime.'

Public executions were abolished two years later.

In the late spring of 1867 the Sultan of Turkey and Ismail Pasha, the Khedive (Viceroy) of Egypt, visited the City of London. A grand dinner and ball were held at the Guildhall in the presence of the Prince of Wales (later Edward VII) and the Duke of Cambridge (later George V). The lord mayor had already given a banquet at the Mansion House for the Khedive which was memorable for the fact that an announcement was made to the effect that the lord mayor would receive a baronetcy and the sheriff would be honoured with a knighthood. The fourteenth Earl of Derby was the one to make the announcement:

'The name of Waterloo itself is hardly more generally known than the name of Alderman Waterlow, and the advantages conferred on the world by that great battle have, I believe, to some extent been equalled by the services which have been conferred upon the City of London by the success of the scheme of Alderman Waterlow for the erection of improved dwellings for the working classes of the metropolis.'

As the relationship between France and the United Kingdom was now on a friendly footing, in June 1867 the lord mayor and sheriff received an invitation from the French authorities to attend the opening of the Paris exhibition on 1 July of that year. The invitation made no mention of the visit being a 'full state' affair and Lord Mayor Gabriel told Sydney that he thought that it would be 'undesirable to go otherwise', and that it was hardly feasible to turn out in Paris in all the civic splendour of London. Sydney had other ideas; he practically insisted that the invitation be accepted and offered to take on the task of ensuring that carriages, horses and liveried servants were safely transported across the Channel, lodged comfortably and returned. The lord mayor could hardly refuse. This was just another example of how seriously Sydney took civic affairs, not only in the administration but also the decorative pomp that goes with them. Sydney was a child of the City and took great pride in all the traditions that it held dear.

Despite the travelling facilities between London and Paris being somewhat primitive, Sydney succeeded in providing the French capital with the pleasure of seeing for the first time a procession with all the full magnificence that was so familiar to London. The streets were crowded with cheering well-wishers and the following day the party was told that the emperor wished to receive them in private audience at the Tuileries Palace the following Sunday. They were shown to the state drawing rooms and, after polite conversation, were introduced to Ismail Pasha who invited them to come and see him at the Elysée Palace the following day. During that meeting the Khedive was anxious to discuss with Sydney various points of commercial interest which were of a fascination to him. Sydney, ever the diplomat, was able to point out to the Khedive that during his reign, trade and commerce between Alexandria and England had increased greatly, largely due to his enlightened policies. This pleased the Khedive so much that he immediately invited both Sydney and the lord mayor to visit him in Egypt. However, they were obliged to explain that this would not be possible during their time in office as it would not be seemly for both the serving lord mayor and the sheriff to be away at the same time exploring the Nile and the Great Pyramids!

However, not long after their terms of office were over the Khedive's agent in London asked Sir Thomas Gabriel and Sydney if they would now be in a position to accept his invitation to visit Egypt; both eagerly accepted. The travelling party consisted of Sir Thomas and Lady Gabriel and two of their daughters, Sir Sydney and Lady Waterlow, their eldest daughter, Ruth, and a Mr J. S. Virtue. The party left London on 17 January 1868, eventually sailing from Marseilles on the P&O steamer *Ripon*. They landed in Malta on 23 January reaching Alexandria four days later. The Khedive sent his chamberlain to meet the party and from that moment until they set sail back to England they were constantly looked after by their host. They were eventually received by the Khedive himself at his palace in Ghizeh when he asked them what they would like to see and do and gave them the use of a steamer to travel on the Nile. At that time, passenger steamers were not permitted to travel the river and so they had to wait some time for the boat to arrive. In the meantime, the party explored Cairo and the Pyramids, and the ladies of the party visited the viceroy's mother in her harem.

When the boat did eventually arrive, they found that it was rather small with barely enough room to accommodate them all; so much so, in fact, that both Sir Thomas Gabriel and Sydney had to be content with sleeping on benches on deck. They travelled to wherever took their fancy, stopping to pick up supplies as required. They saw tombs, temples, sugar factories, mosques and crocodiles, and rode on camels. They returned to Cairo on 27 February, leaving for London on 2 March.

Before the party had left for London, Sydney was contacted by the Foreign Office where an official explained that Sir Thomas ought not to visit the Khedive without also paying a visit to the Sultan. Sydney's answer was that the Khedive had extended the invitation, the Sultan had not. This was not considered a reasonable excuse and that a visit should be arranged immediately. So, before they left Cairo for good, they got aboard a ship bound for Constantinople (Istanbul) which, again, was loaned to them by the ever-generous Khedive. Unfortunately, the local seamanship was not of a particularly high order. The deadlights (portholes) had not been put in and when the wind got up, the best cabins ended up drenched. The error was quickly remedied, and the party were given other cabins where they stayed in bed until their clothes dried.

On arriving in Constantinople, they were told that the Sultan had booked them rooms in the best hotel available. An imperial chamberlain had been assigned to them as a guide and they were offered the use of sedan chairs to take them about the city as well as unrestricted use of the Sultan's box at the opera. The party spent their days sightseeing and towards the end of the trip they were given a banquet by the grand vizier in his palace.

Before they all left, the Sultan sent his chamberlain with a written command conferring the Order of the Medjidieh on both Sir Thomas and Sydney. This order, they were told, bore with it the title of 'Pacha', and that they might, if they saw fit, use that title. Sir Thomas and Lady Gabriel then decided, rather than return directly to England, to travel on to Athens, while Sydney, thinking it was probably about time to go home to see how the business was doing, went via Corfu to Brindisi and on to Florence. He crossed the snow-covered Mont Cenis in a sledge, resting one night in Dijon, another in Paris, finally reaching London after an absence of eleven weeks.

'This was the longest holiday I had ever enjoyed.'

Sydney was now forty-six years of age.

CHAPTER VI
INDUSTRIAL DWELLINGS

For the purposes of this next chapter, it requires the acceptance that the business of Waterlow & Sons had been steadily increasing and would continue to do so year on year to everyone's great satisfaction. However, throughout Sydney's career there was also a constant for which he is, even now, remembered as one of the more prominent features of his public life.

Sydney was one of those men who found it impossible to combine distinct interests and occupations as he feared he would be unable to do full justice to each. He was lucky enough to have a very strong work ethic as well as an extraordinary power of concentration and seemed to have a mind built as if of separate watertight compartments. He would do something to the best of his ability giving it his full attention but then, on completion of the task, would dismiss it entirely from his mind.

Sydney would have never considered himself to be of a socialist persuasion. However, he did have a clear knowledge of the arduous conditions under which too many working men's lives were being lived at the time. He was utterly convinced that the circumstances could be improved, primarily not by charity but by an intelligent application of business principles and methods to matters that where highly prioritised by the working man at that time. He did not think this application of business principles and methods to be primarily anyone else's duty except his. He believed that the conditions in which a man lived affected his character, and he tasked himself to improve the circumstances of the domestic environment of as many working men as possible. On strict business principles, we have already seen what he and his partners did to improve the condition of the thousands who worked for Waterlow & Sons. So, it was with this as a foundation that the Improved Industrial Dwellings Company began its life; a project which, at that time, was one of the most substantial benefits ever conferred on the working classes of London.

Sydney had never regarded himself, nor wished to be regarded by others, as a pioneer in this attempt to improve the dwellings of the 'wage-earning classes' as he preferred to call them. The desperate housing situation had been strongly highlighted twenty years previously by a Dr Southwood Smith and the Rev. W. Denton, Rector of St Bartholomew's Church, Cripplegate, among others. The first company established for this purpose was the *Metropolitan Association for Improving the Dwellings of the Industrial Classes* formed in 1842 under a royal charter, with construction work beginning shortly after. In the years 1854-5 the buildings that this company had erected for families also paid a five per cent dividend, while those for single men returned 3.5 per cent, with even less prior to that. Lady Angela Burdett-Coutts also became involved in very similar projects and, in later years, having ceased building construction on her own account, granted a building lease of land to the Waterlow company near Shoreditch Church on which eighty-eight tenements were erected. These were known as Leopold Buildings.

'Beyond all doubt they [the buildings] stimulated the government of the day in promoting measures, not merely to facilitate that work, but to compel railway companies and others destroying any large number of houses occupied by the poor to provide to a certain extent, new and commodious tenements, suitable for the working classes.'

The principal driving force behind the idea came from the fact that workmen were being turned out of their houses by the railway companies who were tearing old London to pieces to make way for their new thoroughfares across the city. Where were these displaced people to go? There had been private enquiries into the matter along with the insanitary conditions of parts of London, and there had been commissions under the Crown on the matter. Parliament had passed the Public Health Act, but it was a permissive Act and had little effect; the death rate was still excessive. Epidemics which were traceable to the insanitary conditions were responsible for the death of half the children born in the overcrowded districts and cut short the lives of adults by a third.

Sydney's plan was to start small. Securing a piece of ground in Mark Street, Finsbury, he built, at his own expense, four blocks of dwellings. These were divided into flats with external staircases, with rooms for eighty families, or four hundred people, with each tenement being self-contained. The rent charged for these flats was 2/1d per room per week, which would yield a five per cent dividend on the capital invested. Sydney then invited friends to join him in forming a small company with a capital of £50,000 to continue with the enterprise. So began the Improved Industrial Dwellings Company in 1863. By the early 1900s the company was still in existence with a capital holding of over £1,000,000 (£120 million — 2020). Sydney lived long enough to see the building of six thousand tenements distributed throughout the greater part of London; homes for thirty thousand people living in relative comfort and contentment.

Sydney worked out the building details himself, choosing not to use an architect. However, he did employ Matthew Allen as his builder; Allen was the same person who had invented the saddles for the roof telegraph poles for Sydney's original scheme in the City of London. He had recently visited the tenements which had been built in Spitalfields for Lady Angela Burdett-

Coutts and reported back to Sydney with his observations:

'The rooms are well shaped, but how little do the wealthy classes and the architects know of the requirements of the working man? The rooms have only bare whitewashed walls, like the cells of a prison, and the rules prohibit any tenant from knocking in even a nail to hang a picture, or to endeavour to decorate the walls and render the home more cheerful. No one but a working man knows what a working man wants.'

Realising that Allen had clearly thought long and hard about the subject and showed that he very much wanted to help the class to which he belonged, Sydney decided that he was just the man to do the work. Between them they drew up the plans and designs for the properties and also did precisely what an architect, keen to obtain a good effect on the exterior and good decorative effect inside, sometimes omits to do — they considered the probable wishes and the convenience of the tenant. They built scale models out of cardboard including all the furniture cut to scale and arranged in the rooms; they planned a structural arrangement of the fireplaces and windows which would provide the most open and healthy positions with the least exposure to draughts; they never forgot that these were rooms to be lived in, and lived in by people of moderate means of nothing more than their weekly wage.

The general plans were, in some cases, adapted from the model cottage dwellings contributed by Albert, the Prince Consort, to the Great Exhibition of 1851; a model which was re-built in Kennington Park after the Exhibition had finished. However, that particular model had been designed for only two families; Sydney and Matthew Allen's version was to house sixteen. Nevertheless, the principle of the external staircase, which Sydney thought so vital, was taken from Prince Albert's model. It was outside the main walls of the building, and, however placed, was exposed to the fresh air; this also provided a fire escape and limited the risk of infectious or contagious diseases. The ventilation of all the rooms was lateral, each tenement having windows at the front and back allowing a complete flow-through of fresh air when all the windows were opened. The walls and floors, while not fireproof, were so designed as to ensure a maximum delay time in the case of fire. There was a flat roof of light iron girders filled in with concrete and covered with asphalt. The flat roof provided further protection from fire as well as a playground for the children and a drying ground for the wash.

Once the first of the four buildings had been completed, Sydney, anxious to encourage publicity, criticism and suggestions, gave a lunch party on the roof of the structure where a tent was pitched. Attendees included the missionary Lord Radstock, Lord Ebury (Whig politician), Lord Carlingford (Chief Secretary to Ireland and President of the Board of Trade), the social reformer Edwin Chadwick, philanthropist and statesman Samuel Morley and Mr Benjamin Scott the City Chamberlain. There were the usual speeches, most of them to the effect that the first step had now been taken to improve the problem of housing the working classes. The gathered company adopted a resolution that the very best moral and social results were to be expected from such a building, with a good return on the capital invested — a sentiment which would come back to haunt Sydney somewhat unjustly in the years to come.

There was, as there had to be, one dissenting voice. An eminent architect who was present that day voiced his opinion:

'We are summoned here today to inspect and criticise a building of such a novel form of construction that it is beyond all doubt quite a new departure. I do not desire for a moment to review its design in any hostile spirit, but it seems to me that it would be difficult to get a coffin up and down the staircase. The roof upon which we are now enjoying a comfortable luncheon is also a novelty. Still, I must confess that I should not have felt justified in spending the money of any client of mine in the erection of buildings so particular in their arrangement. I nevertheless wish Mr Alderman Waterlow every possible success in carrying out the philanthropic object he has in view.'

There would appear to be an element of sour grapes in this protest, but would the attack have been greater or less if this gentleman had known that a clerk in the office of a local architect had been employed by Sydney to visit the building three or four times a week in order to ensure that the work was carried out correctly and safely? Be that as it may, everyone in the party not connected with that esteemed profession thought that the building was well adapted to purpose. Naturally Sydney was one of them, and he went on to put up three more blocks of the same model without getting an architect involved in any of them. The model went on to stand the test of time with ten such buildings still in use in the twenty-first century, seven of which were constructed while Sydney was still alive. Thirty years after this inaugural completion, Sydney summed up the results of his experience:

'On this important question I am not merely theorising. An experience of thirty years has proved that a fire will not spread from room to room in tenements built on this plan. With nearly six thousand tenements, it was perhaps to be expected that fires should occasionally occur; but on no occasion has the fire ever spread from one tenement to another. Even should this happen, the tenants could always escape freely and without harm by the stone staircase in front of the building, to which all have immediate access from their separate entrance doors.

'This plan of construction was put to a severe test on one occasion, at some buildings in Goswell Street. The tenement houses occupied the frontage of the street. At the southern corner was another street, which ascended rapidly at a right angle. Just in the rear of our block of buildings was an extensive manufactory where there was stored a very large quantity of tallow, oil and other inflammable materials. This factory caught fire one night. The grease melted and poured down the street in liquid flames, setting fire to the shutters of a shop which occupied the corner of our buildings. Over the shop were four floors of tenement dwellings. The shop was occupied by a dealer in india-rubber goods and contained other very inflammable articles. Although the shop was burnt out and completely gutted, the flames, licking up the front and back of the building, broke a few panes of glass and scorched the outside paint, but otherwise did no injury.

'From the same cause — namely, the absence of any vertical flue, like a staircase inside a house — the liability to the spread of contagion is very materially lessened. On more than one occasion, when there was an epidemic of smallpox in London, and the disease was brought home to our buildings by children attending the elementary schools, it never spread amongst the tenants. It was most satisfactory to find that the death and disease rate, among the thirty thousand persons who live in the blocks of buildings belonging to my company in various parts of the metropolis, was, in the year 1896, only 9.9 per one thousand. The average death-rate in London for the same period was 18.5 and no doubt the death-rate in the poorer quarters of the metropolis would be thirty or forty per one thousand. This is, I trust, sufficient evidence of the validity of my statements as to the immunity of our buildings from the spread of contagious disease.'

As the idea behind the scheme was that returns, such as they were, would be coming from the very moderate rents charged to the tenants, economy of construction was studied carefully at every point. One of the cost savings introduced was in the use of a new building material which was twenty-five per cent cheaper than stone or brick. The arches and lintels throughout the buildings were supplied and fixed in place at a cost no greater than the labour costs alone would have been had ordinary brick arches been installed. This revolutionary material had been developed by Matthew Allen and was later widely used by other builders in London. Allen, who did not have the benefit of a great education, had read the report of a lecture given at the Institute of Civil Engineers by the eminent architect Sydney Smirke RA who had studied the concrete used in old Italian and Roman buildings. He had found that it was composed of Roman cement mixed with broken lava from Mount Vesuvius. When combined, the cement entered the pores in the lava, and it was discovered that the resulting material would not split. Matthew Allen then took this one stage further, reasoning that there ought to be a substitute in Britain for the Vesuvius lava; he found what he was looking for in waste coke. This new concrete was then manufactured using four parts small drift coke to one part of Portland cement, strengthened, where necessary, with wrought iron.

When the building project began high rents for cheap lodgings were the norm in London. For the tenants of these new buildings the rents were fixed at between 5/- and 6/6d per week. The sum of the rents from the first four buildings amounted to £309; the expenditure in ground rent, rates, insurance and repairs was £125; balance £184 — over nine per cent.

The four blocks in Finsbury cost Sydney £10,000 (£1.2 million) and he did not ask for any financial assistance until the work had been completed. He does not seem to have initially thought that any considerable re-housing of the working classes could be accomplished by private enterprise. But now, having demonstrated the possibility, he decided that a larger project should be undertaken to show as an example to the country. He approached his friends for additional funding, some £25,000, and received subscriptions from fourteen people. The largest investor was Sir Henry Edwards, MP for Weymouth, who donated £5,000. Lord Stanley, later Earl of Derby, became chairman of the board of directors with Sydney as deputy chairman, George Goschen, later Viscount Goschen, Samuel Morley, a woollen goods manufacturer and philanthropist, and others also became directors. The company started life without an office, board meetings being held in the counting house of Waterlow & Sons. Lord Stanley remained chairman until 1866 when he accepted an office in the Cabinet; Sydney was then chosen as his successor and remained in office for thirty years.

With the first £25,000 having been spent to the satisfaction of the board, it was resolved to increase the capital to £50,000. This was raised again to £100,000 and then again to £500,000 with power to borrow on a first mortgage from the Public Works Loan Commissioners of another £500,000. In order to raise the first £500,000, it was necessary to make an appeal to the public. The take-up was slow at first but the appeal of the expectation of a five per cent return on the investment soon sparked interest and the money was soon forthcoming.

In the meantime, Sydney attempted to persuade the Common Council to do a share of the work in providing improved housing for the labouring poor. There was at that time a Finsbury Surplus Estate Fund amounting to over £42,000 which had been earmarked for such a purpose. However, nothing was being done with the money and so in October 1862 Sydney began an enquiry into the fund and the destruction of the houses of the industrial poor in the City of London, and whether this fund could be used for supplying new homes. The money had been available for use since 1851 and land had already been bought, but at that stage various experiments that had been performed had brought about discouraging results and the land was sold again eight years later. The City of London Police had made representation to the court pointing out the difficulty they had in obtaining lodgings and the petition was signed by 470 men of the force, eighty of whom had families with up to four children and who were occupying single rooms at 4/- per week. Sydney's statement to the court was full and convincing and his resolution was adopted. A committee was appointed and within two years the court had built a large block in Farringdon Road known as Corporation Buildings; others were also erected later near Holborn. By 1863 they had spent £105,000 in the building of 1,003 rooms with an average net return of 4 per cent.

While this was considered an excellent result, there was also a further reaching service which the Corporation can be credited with. They had now taken and maintained a position of co-operation in the general movement for the better housing of the working classes. It became more and more difficult for outside corporate interests, eager for the destruction of the houses in order to free up land for other projects, to destroy property without rebuilding, now that the City of London had declared itself to be on the side of the working men and their families. Nevertheless, Sydney knew that a long, hard struggle lay before him. The company continued to prosper, money was coming in and buildings were going up. However, there was always a battle to be fought with the railways and other companies focused on the acquisition of land, seemingly too often unconcerned about the people they dispossessed. The problem was not only to re-house them, but to do so within a reasonable distance of their place of work. Occasionally, this was eased by the extension of the railway system into the suburbs, but the overall problem was far from being resolved. The struggle continued for over twenty years in Parliament, the press, various boardrooms and even in Cabinet ministers' offices.

At the forefront of all this — Sydney. Public opinion was now so aroused on the subject that he was assured of good support. The press was on his side, as was the House of Commons — generally speaking. Boards of directors, who existed solely to promote the interests of their shareholders, eventually came around to the idea that it would be expedient to take notice of public opinion. Cabinet ministers, to whom public opinion had never been a matter of indifference, concluded that it would gladly support the expenditure of public money for a cause which only a few years before would have been thought impracticable and fanciful. The five per cent dividend of the Improved Industrial Dwellings Company had converted even the most sceptical.

Sydney's arguments had proved to be difficult to refute or neglect. The work of destroying homes for the development of the railways would never have continued without the sanction of Parliament. It was certainly Parliament's responsibility to make provision for the many thousands of working men and their families for whom it would mean much distress, if not total ruin. However, there had now come a point that Sydney had persuaded everyone he could provide funds for the project from his friends, public subscription and the Common Council. The situation was such that it was clear that more money was urgently needed and more than could be expected from individuals. It had required a great deal of effort to reach the sums already secured; however, the need was pressing as the expansion of the railways and other essential construction projects were continuing on a scale much greater than had been anticipated, and once the great areas of housing had been cleared for these projects the difficulties multiplied exponentially. It had now reached the stage where state aid in some form or other was required as soon as possible.

So, Sydney began the next stage in his usual modest way. On 7 April 1865 he wrote to Frederick Peel, Secretary to the Treasury, setting out the facts and laying down what he believed to be the government's obligations. The letter laid down a proposal that Mr Peel should bring the problem to the attention of the Chancellor of the Exchequer and to ask whether he would be willing to receive a deputation with a view to discussing the principle of the scheme.

The Chancellor at the time was William Gladstone; however, Gladstone's name does not seem to appear in relation to the subsequent proceedings in the matter, so it is entirely possible that he was too busy with more pressing duties and so was unable to give Sydney's proposal any attention. The scheme was quite simple; it required an Act of Parliament empowering the Public Works Loan Commissioner to grant loans upon mortgage of lands and houses applied to the use and occupation of the working classes, with all due specified precautions and securities. Sydney, optimistic in his official inexperience, asked for an appointment for the proposed interview before or as soon as possible after Easter. Peel sent his reply on 15 May stating that he had been commanded by the Lords Commissioners of Her Majesty's Treasury to inform Sydney that "their Lordships doubt whether public aid could be given to any such company unless the rate of profit were so limited as to distinguish their case from that of an ordinary commercial enterprise".

Sydney replied that the company would happily agree to five per cent as opposed to the usual ten per cent on landed property. On 14 June the Lords Commissioners reply saying that they agree to this and promise to ask Parliament for the necessary authority. Unfortunately, Parliament was shortly due to be dissolved and so nothing more could be done that year. Nevertheless, the Act was subsequently passed and by 1897 the loans received by the Improved Industrial Dwellings Company from the Public Works Loan Commissioners amounted to £484,000 of which £173,000 had been repaid. The company's capital stood at £500,000 stock and £165,000 in deferred shares of £1 each, all fully paid. The total expenditure on land and buildings had been £1,112,242 including part of the reserve funds used in extending the company's work. A dividend of five per cent per annum was paid regularly on stock and deferred shares.

Between the date of the first application for public money and 1897 the work of erecting dwellings and protecting the interests of the working classes had encountered many different obstacles. In a letter to *The Times* newspaper dated 14 April 1872, Sydney drew attention to several bills then before Parliament for the construction of new streets. The Metropolitan Board of Works and the projectors of the Mid-London Railway proposed to demolish 1,152 houses leaving 3,870 people homeless. As before, the powers granted by the bills to destroy these properties were compulsory with the powers to re-build being permissive only. Once again, Sydney set out his reasoned arguments adding:

'There are other reasons, social, political and moral, why it is to the very highest degree undesirable that workmen should be driven from the localities in which their labour found remunerative employment. But if compulsory powers for the destruction of their houses are to be given, and only permissive and inoperative powers of reconstruction, the evils both of scattering and of overcrowding will ensue. There is, I think, one method of avoiding these evils, and my object in writing this letter is to bring that method prominently before the public, and to urge its adoption. The power which is compulsory in the one case should be made compulsory in the other. Parliament must be asked, not only to give power to pull down these houses, but to impose on those who exercise that power the correlative responsibility of erecting improved dwellings of the same class in their place. I venture, therefore, to suggest that clauses should be inserted in the bill promoted by the Metropolitan Board of Works requiring them to set aside out of the surplus funds, which will remain after the construction of the proposed new streets, or out of any surplus lands now in the possession of the board, a number of sites on which tenement houses suitable for the working classes may be built. The area thus set aside should be sufficient for the erection of dwellings to accommodate all the persons who may be displaced.'

The Times newspaper, however, sided with the railways and the Board of Works and advised Parliament to fall back on general principles: "that is, an improved street and building legislation in order to obtain wider thoroughfares, better cleanliness and less crowding". As for the railways, they were having a hard time of it and were having to dispose of their surplus land for the best prices they could get. *The Times* again went on the offensive:

'How will they like to be compelled to restrict themselves to the limited and capricious market of philanthropists, building houses for poor people on the bare chance of five per cent returns? We believe that London will always find space enough for her increasing millions. Space increases as the square of the distance from the centre; and even if the entire heart of the metropolis were covered with public buildings, railway stations, manufactories, banks and offices, the only difference need be that the persons employed in them would have to go half a mile farther to more wholesome dwellings.'

Fortunately, there were those influential people who supported Sydney in his views, Lord Lyttelton and Lord Shaftesbury among them, and they brought with them other newspapers in their support. Sydney also restated his case in the *Daily News*, being blunt in his reply to the objection that he did not provide single rooms:

'It is quite true that I do not provide single rooms. But one of the objects of these improved dwellings is to help eradicate the whole system of living of which these single-room dwellings are the evil sign. We build for the future and look forward to the time when no family need be compelled to live in a single room. It is impossible that either sanitary or moral conditions can ever be satisfied under such a system. No proper feeling of decency or self-respect can be cultivated in families living in a single room.

'Yet even the unfortunate class whom overcrowding forces into single-room dwellings are helped and relieved by the provision of more eligible tenements. The better class of working people are glad to get out of such miserable dwellings into better ones, and, as they do so, more room is left for the rest. It is the competition of better-class workmen with the very poor which makes the rent of bad dwellings in backstreets so very high. Diminish that competition, and rents will fall, and the owners of such property will be compelled by the loss of tenants to effect improvements which will never be accomplished in any other way.

'Improvements of this kind must begin from the top. If you simply draw out the worst layer from below, those above will sink into its place; while by taking away the upper strata, those below, relieved from the pressure, rise into their vacant places. Even the poor widow who can only pay two shillings a week for a single room is thus most directly benefited by the provision of these improved dwellings. She gets a better room for her money when the keenest competitors for it have been housed elsewhere.'

The subject became more and more complicated by well-meant but ill-judged efforts towards reform. Sydney let it be known that he thought that:

'the gravest obstacle to the improvement of the dwellings of the working classes lay in the course taken by the Metropolitan Board of Works in carrying out the Artisans' Dwellings Act.'

So, when the Metropolitan Streets Improvement Act was before the House of Commons in 1872, he found that, as with railway bills, this Act gave full powers for the destruction of workmen's dwellings without insisting on the building of new accommodation. After much persistence and letter writing, he finally secured the insertion of Clause 49, in which was embodied the principle, or the germ of it, that those who demolish workmen's houses must set apart certain land for their reconstruction.

By this time, and even two years later in 1874, the question of obtaining land was becoming more difficult than the question of money for building. Sydney was becoming more and more convinced that the public were ready to find any amount of money to carry on the work, especially as he himself had nearly £250,000 under his control for the purpose. He wrote in another letter to *The Times*:

'We are, however, all working with our hands tied. We cannot obtain possession of the fever-dens in our narrow courts and alleys and are practically unable to secure sites in the required localities. The good work has hitherto been carried on mainly through the facilities afforded by the Duke of Westminster, the Baroness Burdett-Coutts, the Marquis of Northampton, the Rev. W. Bassett, the ecclesiastical commissioners, and other large landowners in the metropolis. One of these proprietors sold to us a few years since nine acres of small, dilapidated houses in the East End of London, two public houses being the only substantial buildings on the property. The School Board have built and opened a school for 1,500 children on one plot. New houses in flats of four or five stories have been erected, and in a few years every sign of the old houses will be gone. This was a rare chance which may never occur again.

'Parliament must impose on some public metropolitan body the responsibility and the power to purchase by compulsion, not merely the house property declared by the sanitary authority to be unfit for human habitation, but also the houses and lands adjacent thereto, in order that suitable sites with proper approaches may be secured. The ground when cleared by the public authority should be let by tender on long building leases, with stringent provisions for the erection and maintenance of workmen's dwellings on plans to be approved by the lessors.'

Sydney went on to admit that the ground rent obtained would not be equal in all cases to the cost of the improvement and he suggested that the money should be raised by the issue of 3.5 per cent metropolitan consols. In that case the loss would be comparatively small, and more than covered by the levy of a farthing rate on the assessment of the metropolis. This in turn would be recouped to the ratepayers by the consequential saving on the reduction of the death and disease rate among the working population. The fact that it would be reduced may be inferred from the fact that the death rate in the improved dwellings was, in 1872, only 15.8 per 1,000 people as compared generally in the metropolis of 25.5 per 1,000; while the average death rate for ten years in the improved dwellings was sixteen as opposed to twenty-four in the whole of the metropolis.

The subject was brought before the House of Commons in 1874, Benjamin Disraeli now being prime minister. Sir Ughtred Shuttleworth moved a resolution affirming the necessity of providing better dwellings for the working classes in London. Sydney, by now an MP himself, also spoke on the resolution, urging for the levy of a rate of 1d for the purpose and advocating it upon economical as well as medical and sanitary grounds. The resolution was withdrawn, but the change in the attitude of the authorities was noticeable when, in October, the Home Secretary, Richard Cross, asked Sydney to supply him with further information and suggestions for improvement and he used this opportunity to again urge the granting of compulsory powers. It clearly must have had some effect as in 1875 the Artisans' Dwelling Bill was introduced.

'I rejoice to find that the government have taken the matter in hand so promptly, and with a clear and evident desire to deal with it practically and effectually.'

But he issued a memorandum pointing out the need for certain amendments. Here was the old problem raising its head again; it was, to a great extent, a permissive bill and the district medical officer possessed the influence to make it operative or inoperative. There were also many other criticisms which the passage of time has borne out. When the bill came on, Sydney moved an amendment for referring to arbitration differences between the local authority and the intending purchaser of lands. But the Home Secretary said it would delay the sale of land for twelve to eighteen months and the bill was acceptable as it stood. A Mr Fawcett told Richard Cross that if he insisted with the clause as written then the Act would be a dead letter; Cross would not give way. The amendment was rejected, and the bill was passed with the result that the Board of Works interpreted its duty in such a way that there continued to be neglect and delay which the amendment was intended to prevent.

At the annual meeting of the Improved Industrial Dwellings Company in October 1875, Sydney, as Chairman, announced that the company must issue 25,000 additional £10 shares. This would bring the capital up to £500,000 and, with their borrowing powers, this brought the company's financial resources to nearly £1,000,000. A writer in one journal even went so far as to say:

'The chairman of this most business-like yet eminently benevolent concern has probably done more than all the temperance lecturers in the land to effect a real reform in the habits and morals of the working classes.'

What was even more gratifying was that the workmen themselves were eager to occupy the properties. Sydney reported that:

'On several occasions during the past year there had not been a single tenement to let on a Saturday

85

night, and the majority of applications came from old tenants.

'Each new building scheme, whether in Westminster, City Road, Pimlico, Islington, Shoreditch, Holborn or elsewhere, represents an oasis of wholesomeness in some dirty desert of dingy and rickety buildings, where the toiling millions are at present worse housed than the rich man's horse, ox, or ass.'

In other cities there was similar work going on. Glasgow and Edinburgh were prime examples where intelligent effort was being made towards better housing for the working classes, and Glasgow supplied Sydney with one of his most effective answers to the Metropolitan Board of Works. In 1877 a House of Commons Committee reported that:

'delay had occurred, and was likely to occur, in providing dwellings for labourers unhoused by street improvements, on the lands which it is provided shall be set apart for them by the Metropolitan Board of Works.'

The board then had a Street Improvements Bill before the house which proposed to displace 25,000 people of the labouring class and to provide for the re-housing of only 2,750, the evidence being supplied by Sir Joseph Bazalgette. Sydney showed how the Act of 1872 had been worked and the board expressed a fear that his statements might give the impression that they were defeating the intentions of the legislature to facilitate the building of dwellings for the working classes. "That," said Sydney, "is the very essence of my complaint." He did not complain that the land had not been sold to his company but that it had not been let or sold to anyone.

The whole matter came before the House of Commons again in 1881 when Sir Ughtred Shuttleworth proposed, seconded by Sydney, a resolution for a select committee to consider the working of the Artisans' Dwellings Act of 1875 and Metropolitan Street Improvement Acts of 1872 and 1877:

'and especially, to enquire into the causes that have prevented the reconstruction of dwellings for the poorer classes to the extent contemplated and authorised by these three Acts of Parliament.'

The superintending architect of the Board of Works, in anticipation of this, or in reply to an earlier criticism, had stated that the estimated cost of sites was £735,000 and that the price offered by the Peabody Trustees had caused a loss to the ratepayer of £562,061. However, Sydney showed that, reckoning the land used for street improvements, reserved for commercial purposes, sold to the Peabody Trustees, required for the increased open spaces and the increased value of the assessment of the new buildings, there was a balance on the debit side not of £562,061 but of £158,862. He then showed that for this sum London had secured two great advantages; firstly, the saving to the poor rates by the decrease of death and disease, and secondly, the decrease of the risk of the spread of contagious diseases by stamping out the fever-dens in the overcrowded districts. Analysing the figures, he further showed that, upon the usual basis of calculation and proportion of deaths to causes of illness averaging three weeks, and assuming that each sick person cost the ratepayers 16s a week, there had been a direct monetary saving of £11,520 per annum. This, capitalised at five per cent, amounted to £220,400 against the £158,862 standing to the debit of the cost account for clearing these sites.

Sydney persisted with his queries to the Board of Works. He wanted to know why there had been such a poor showing when so much power had been granted under the three Acts, while Glasgow and Edinburgh had carried out similar Acts with great advantage to the people of the respective cities and at a very small cost to the ratepayers. Glasgow had spent £2,000,000 but with only a cost to the ratepayers of £300,000. London had spent a similar sum with the ratepayers having to find a far greater sum. There was no satisfactory answer forthcoming from either the press or the House of Commons Committee.

In 1884 the Improved Industrial Dwellings Company celebrated its coming of age by the opening of the Sandringham Buildings in Soho. The Prince of Wales, President for the day, presented to Sydney on behalf of the shareholders a service of plate costing 1,000 guineas. The prince said:

'In common with all those who are interested in this very important subject, my best thanks are due to you, Sir Sydney Waterlow, and to your able colleagues, who have come forward in the most generous and disinterested spirit to devote your valuable time, perfectly gratuitously, to the furtherance of this object. We are very glad that an opportunity has been given us of assisting at the presentation of these works of art, and of testifying, by our presence here today, the deep sense of gratitude which we all entertain towards you for your unwearied and unceasing labours in this excellent and philanthropic work.'

It has been mentioned many times that Sydney always rejected the idea of being called a philanthropist. Despite dedicating twenty years of his life to such honourable work he did not consider himself worthy of the title. He knew how valuable the work was and was glad and grateful to receive the gifts from the shareholders and the generous eulogy from the Prince of Wales. However, from the start he was keen to push the business side of the whole enterprise and to dwell as little as possible on the benevolent aspect as he knew how easily the sensitiveness and pride of the classes he wished to benefit would be offended. He knew that his tenants liked to believe they were paying the market value of the tenements they were hiring, which they were. There was no room for any sense of dependence or of favour conferred. Sydney felt that he was only discharging his duty as a useful citizen of the City of

London. He had been an apprentice and a working printer, and this allowed him to empathise with what men in that position of life would feel.

'If you want to help them, you must do it on even terms. Charity is not a thing the British working men will ask for, nor, save in the extremity, accept.'

Even today, at the time of writing, there are ten of the original buildings still being occupied. Most of them no longer accommodate the same social class for whom they were originally intended, but they stand as a testimony to the man who wanted to improve the lot of the working classes of London. They are monuments to him; they are legacies to the City he loved.

CHAPTER VII
POLITICS & PARLIAMENT

Although Sydney devoted a great deal of his time to political involvement both within the City of London and the country as a whole, it was never to become the main focus of his life. Nevertheless, this element of his career was a significant part of who he was, and so it would be remiss not to make reference to it.

Sydney was a staunch Liberal, but although he took the politics of the country in all seriousness, he also saw membership of the House of Commons as yet another means of promoting the causes close to his heart. When he first began to concern himself with parliamentary contests, the City of London was already a Liberal stronghold and returned four members of that party to Westminster. In the general election of 1852, the leader of the party was Lord John Russell who was standing for one of the seats within the City. Sydney devoted as much time as business would allow to work for the Liberal leader during the election. The City itself was beginning to turn quickly in favour of the Tories, and Sydney felt he should do all he could to stem the tide. However, the growth of Waterlow & Sons at that time was such that it required most of Sydney's time and energy and that whatever time was spent during the day in the service of the Whig cause had to be made up by night-work for the business. It is unlikely that much of Sydney's effort had any real influence on the eventual outcome as Russell was elected, not because he was a Liberal but because he was Lord John. Nevertheless, Sydney's experience served to raise many questions within him and his general interest in politics began to grow.

Political passions were beginning to run high in Westminster and, as history is keen to relate, there was much heated debate between Messrs Gladstone and Disraeli on many topics, none more explosive than the resolution for the disestablishment of the Irish Church. By the time a general election was called in 1868, Sydney decided that the time had now come to dip his toe into the water of national politics.

Between 1868 and 1885 Sydney fought eight different contested elections, winning four and losing four. Dumfriesshire was the first and certainly the most memorable, and it was indeed the hand of fate which guided him there initially. He had sent his secretary, Aldous Mays, to the London Institution in Finsbury Circus, London, to look for certain information. While looking through *The Scotsman* newspaper, Mays noted that the Liberals of Dumfriesshire were looking for a candidate to stand for them in the constituency and so he suggested to Sydney that this could be a good opportunity for him. Sydney said that he had never even been to Scotland before and that he would be an unknown quantity there; but Mays persisted:

'Give me a ten-pound note and let me go to Dumfries and see what the chances are.'

Mays' report was so encouraging that Sydney resolved to stand if the Liberals would have him. He travelled up by the night mail on 20 October 1868, arriving the following morning, and was addressing a meeting of the electors at two o'clock that afternoon.

The nature of the encouraging information that the zealous Mr Hays had obtained can only be guessed at. At that time Dumfriesshire was a pocket constituency; it belonged to the Duke of Buccleuch and he, his father and grandfather before him had been nominated and elected as Members of Parliament for the county for the past eighty years, and there had been no contest for the seat in all that time. It was scarcely supposed that it would be possible to proffer a strong contention against the seemingly all-powerful aristocrat. Nevertheless, Sydney entered the fray with his usual determination and vigour, and right from the start became acutely aware of the concept of heckling. He was asked whether he would vote for an Eight Hours Bill, and after initially explaining that he himself had worked for weekly wages and had a deep sympathy with the working man, he continued:

'I would say to my friend, and I would say to the working man of this country, if you want to limit yourselves to eight hours' pay, well, then, Parliament should let you do so if you like. But I ask you not to take away from your neighbour the right to work ten hours if he likes. No man should endeavour to restrict the hours of labour for his fellow workmen.'

This was something from which he never swerved his entire life.

Nothing could better show the state of affairs in Dumfriesshire than the fact that there was no register of voters. Those who should have been responsible to have drawn it up never even thought that it would be needed, or that anybody would venture to oppose the will or the nomination of the Duke of Buccleuch. What was the use of a register of voters when nobody voted? There was not a single man who had ever exercised his right to vote in the county.

Yet all the methods of pressurising a constituency's voters seem to have been well known to the duke and his agents, and these were all relentlessly put into force; the tyranny of the open vote was in full operation. The duke scornfully repelled the charge that he would unduly influence his tenants. But the officers and bailiffs on his estates were putting every kind of pressure on the tenants to vote for Major Walker, the Tory candidate. The same was also happening on the estates of Sir John Heron Maxwell. In order to be able to hold meetings for the Liberal cause the local Presbyterian church was pressed into service. When Sydney returned home one Sunday to deal with personal affairs a detective was employed by the Tories to follow him to see what church service he attended. As soon as it was known that he was a Unitarian he was denounced and ridiculed all over Dumfriesshire. It was almost a copybook occurrence of his experience when standing for election as a City alderman. The duke's agents were, quite naturally, mortified and denied any of it had taken place even when Sydney stood on the platform with two brownish-pink slips of paper in his hand and read out the telegrams they had sent to the detective in question. Polling day came on the 1 November of that year. An hour after the polls closed, the result was announced:

Waterlow 1,100

Walker 1,056

It was a great victory, and one of the most notable of the election which also saw William Gladstone returned to Westminster with a majority of 128. The influence and power of the Buccleuchs in Scotland had been shaken. However, it had taken someone with the resource, courage and spirit of Sydney to ensure the result.

Unfortunately, it was not long before it was discovered that Waterlow & Sons held government contracts, but Sydney was at great pains to point out that the partnership with his brothers had expired, and that he had no share in the profits of the firm. Nevertheless, it was finally decided by the lawyers and a parliamentary committee that as the government had not released him from liability in the event of his brothers failing to perform their contracts Sydney could not keep

95

his seat and he was forced to resign. A fresh election was held; regrettably, this time, the circumstances were less than favourable. The Duke of Buccleuch and Sir John Heron Maxwell were reinforced by the Marquis of Queensbury and a Mr Jardine. Queensbury had been promised a seat in the House of Lords as representative peer in Scotland and spent the whole day at the polling booth watching every voter as they came to vote. In the end the result stood as:

Walker 1,117

Waterlow 1,081

Six more years of government under William Gladstone passed, to be followed by the general election of 1874. Not deterred by his previous experiences, Sydney stood for election again, this time in Maidstone, along with Sir John Lubbock; by way of fate, both candidates were returned with large majorities. Despite now being a Member of Parliament for his party, Sydney was quick to point out that he did not always agree with Gladstone's way of thinking. However, he was happy to acknowledge that the prime minister was responsible for passing more beneficial measures than many others before him. He thought that the Irish Church Act and the Irish Land Act opened a new era in legislation; something that the Tories actually agreed with. Also, the Army Regulation Bill "for the first time gave the British Army to the British people". The new Ballot Bill "for the first time in the history of the country Englishmen will be able to vote as they like, none daring to make them afraid". Finally, the University Tests Act "has simply thrown open the universities to the whole nation" and he looked forward to the day when all antiquated restrictions and privileges should be abolished, and the universities would be free to all students.

In the general election of 1880 both Sydney and Sir John Lubbock lost their Maidstone seats. However, Lubbock was returned by the University of London as their MP and Sydney was put forward as the Liberal candidate in nearby Gravesend. His opponent was the third Sir Robert Peel, son of the former prime minister, who was determined to bring Sydney's religious affiliations to the attention of the voting population just as had been done in Dumfriesshire twelve years earlier. Fortunately for Sydney, the people of Gravesend ignored Peel's arguments and he was returned to Parliament with a large majority. He remained as the borough's MP for five years and was considered to have done good work although he never exactly became a standout politician. He was successful in amending the Thames River Bill which affected concerns of his constituents, and the Alkali Bill which had consequences regarding the large cement works in the borough.

Then came the general election of 1885, and Sydney gave some consideration as to if and where he might stand for re-election. He was in the process of buying his future home, Trosley Towers, near Wrotham in mid-Kent and became torn between continuing to represent Gravesend or to move further south into the county. Sydney had been successful in delivering the right to vote to the agricultural labourer, but it was still uncertain as to how this freshly enfranchised group of society was going to use its newfound power. There was only one way to find out and this was exactly what Sydney had resolved to do. However, not for the first time, the new voters showed themselves to be very timid when it came to exercising their rights. Old influences were still strong, and the landlords and local parsons had not lost their influence. However, Sydney was certainly a reformer; he wanted to ensure that the rights of tenant farmers were recognised and respected. He advocated compensation for tenants' improvements, and he supported the disestablishment of the Church of England as a means of enlarging the usefulness of the Church. The local clergy responded to this by asking the voters if they wished to see Canterbury Cathedral turned into a museum and withdrew their custom from local tradespeople and shopkeepers who showed any affiliation with Liberalism. Sydney was quick to counter:

'During the last four or five months I have been negotiating for a property in this county, and, as a temptation to purchase more than I wanted, I was offered the right of appointing a minister of the Church of England in two parishes.'

It was common knowledge that Sydney was a committed Unitarian, but he was still offered the right of appointment for a religion he did not follow. This, he felt, weakened the Church and he was able to repeat the testimony of one of the archbishops given a couple of days previously "that a man who desires to strengthen the Church should see to some of these reforms". Unfortunately, all this discourse did not serve to strengthen his cause; Sydney lost the election along with all the other Liberal candidates in Kent. He managed to poll more votes than any other of his Liberal brothers, but it was not to be.

It was now clear to Sydney that he could make better use of the remaining working years of his life rather than sitting in Parliament or contesting seats in elections. He was now sixty-three years of age and had his hands full with both public and private business. It was evident that the more meaningful parts of his life were to be found elsewhere other than the House of Commons, and had he spent his whole career solely as an MP then there is a very good chance that his life would have been nowhere near as spectacular as it was. The history of the House of Commons could very easily be written without even mentioning his name and he was all too well aware of that. So, after his defeat in mid-Kent he turned his attention to endeavours where he knew he could make a worthwhile impact.

CHAPTER VIII
LORD MAYOR OF LONDON

It is safe to say that Sydney considered his term of office as lord mayor to be the pinnacle of his career. He had already totally devoted himself to the offices of alderman and sheriff, and so the next step up to lord mayor was the final stage in the natural sequence of events. In Sydney's case there was no question as to his suitability for the post, and there was certainly no opposition to his selection as his name was first on the list sent by the livery to the Court of Aldermen and he was chosen lord mayor on Saturday 28 September 1872. One question, the only one, he was asked by a liveryman in the Common Hall was whether, if elected, he would do what lay in him to promote technical education by means of the action of the livery companies; this he promised to do whether in or out of office, a pledge he upheld for more than twenty years.

His first duty upon election was to make a speech of thanks to the Court of Aldermen for choosing him, to compliment his predecessor and others before him, and to offer the court an assurance that all his time, energy and means would be devoted to the fulfilling of his new duties.

'The lord mayor is the elected chief of the Livery of London. He is the representative of the principal of popular election and is bound to defend that principal to the utmost.

'You, the Livery of London, have placed in my keeping the honour and credit of the oldest, the most venerable, and the greatest, of the municipal institutions of the country — indeed, I might add, of the world. It will be my earnest care that that honour and that credit shall not suffer in my hands.

'But we live in days when the most time-honoured institutions have to justify their existence by proof of the advantages which they confer on the people of the present day. The municipality of the City of London continually gives such proof, not only on its own behalf, but in support of municipal institutions throughout the country.'

His duties, ceremonial and executive, began immediately. If anyone had thought that this hard-headed, energetic man of business was merely going to be a figurehead or was just going to content himself with the ornamental functions of the position or with the routine work of the office, they were going to be very much mistaken.

The Corporation of London is an association of guilds which was formed for the safety, security and advancement of trade and commerce. So, in October 1872 Sydney, as lord mayor elect, found himself as the guest of the cutlers of Sheffield:

'You will understand that we are not associated so much for the mere purpose of trading as for the maintenance of the honour, reputation and best interests of traders.'

At Westminster Hall, on 8 November, Lord Chancellor Selborne signified Queen Victoria's approval of the election:

'The City of London has never been behindhand in fostering useful undertakings at home — such as those connected with the development of industrial houses and middle-class schools. More than all, you, Sir Sydney, have shown yourself a man beyond other men, apt for a position in which such works have to be done. You have been honourably distinguished — so honourably that, even if the City had not accumulated honours upon you, your name ought to be remembered with praise and gratitude hereafter for the efforts you have already made to improve the condition and the dwellings of the working classes — an undertaking of the most vital importance, which, if crowned with success, will set an example which I hope will be followed throughout the land.'

It was clear that the election of a Unitarian lord mayor was not going to be regarded as a threat to Church or state. Sydney obviously did not think so either, appointing the Rev. William Rogers, Rector of Bishopsgate, to be his chaplain. Rogers was a clergyman of the Church of England who took broad views of his office as a minister of religion and this served to substantiate Sydney's way of thinking.

Sydney's journal contains entries in which he records his personal opinions, impressions and emotions with total freedom and sincerity:

'I naturally look back on November 9, 1872, as one of the most important days in my life, for on this day I was to make my public appearance amongst the citizens as their new lord mayor and chief magistrate of our great City. I could not resist feeling considerable anxiety as to how the day would pass off, for I had to show myself, not only to the Barons of the Exchequer at Westminster, but to the vast multitude who thronged the streets through which the ancient pageant and cavalcade customary on such occasions had to pass.'

This spectacular show has been independently described many times in the past and nowadays we are annually invited to watch it in the comfort of our homes as it is broadcast live on television. However, it is scarce that the procession would have been described first hand by its principal participant:

'Fortunately for me, the weather was very fine, and the day being Saturday, with its usual half-holiday, there was naturally a much larger crowd in every direction than I had ever before seen in the streets of London. Brilliant equipages, gorgeous uniforms, and horses prancing to brass bands, were main features in the panorama which hundreds of thousands of people thronged to witness.

'From the time I left Guildhall at one o'clock until I returned to the point of my departure at four o'clock, my reception was most enthusiastic, and materially helped to sustain my courage for the duties and responsibilities of the banquet which was to follow at the Guildhall at seven o'clock. The enthusiasm of the crowds which came out to see the show was by no means confined to that part of the City in which I had resided and carried on my business for so many years, or to the thoroughfares within the City walls. From Temple Bar to Charing Cross the roadway and the pavements contained a crowded multitude of good-natured men and women, joyously shouting in the sunshine. On reaching Charing Cross, I found the whole space from Northumberland Avenue to the bottom of Pall Mall, and the rising ground up to the National Gallery, a mass of moving hats and bonnets, diversified by heads without either.

'On reaching the Courts of the Exchequer, I had to claim at the hands of the learned Barons the acknowledgement of the full, free, and ancient privileges accorded to lord mayors of the City of London. Their lordships at once granted them in complimentary terms.

'On returning from the presentation to the Barons of the Exchequer, down the New Embankment, the crowd had in no degree lessened. Cheers and congratulations were heard on all sides, varied by boys shouting, "Portrait of the new lord mayor, only a penny!" and other cries. The people were mostly orderly in their deportment, having, no doubt, come out of their homes to witness the proceedings of the day, not so much from reverence for the incoming lord mayor and the Corporation, as from motives of curiosity to view the pomp and circumstance which characterised the time-honoured display.'

For the Guildhall banquet in the evening the new library was available for the first time as a reception room for all the guests, but Sydney is less than forthcoming with his thoughts and impressions of the event and the speeches. He records the fact that he was disappointed by the absence of Mr Gladstone, "owing to indisposition and the need of rest to prepare him for the duties of the ensuing session", and possibly also due to the ongoing by-elections at that time. The new lord mayor's health was finally proposed by Lord Granville:

'I propose it to you on account of his personal character. I propose it to you on account of the labours he has had in the service of the poor, and, if I may say so, I am encouraged to add that I propose it for the dignity and tact with which he has conducted the proceedings of this gorgeous banquet.'

Proposing the health of the lady mayoress:

'It has often been said that the influence of women is in exact proportion to the progress of civilisation. I believe it was in this great banqueting hall that the example was first set of public dinners where men need not be separated for many hours from the society of those who give grace and brilliancy to the scene.'

Being the astute businessman, it didn't take Sydney long to calculate "the total expenses of the day's proceedings" at £3,300, of which half was paid by the lord mayor himself and a quarter by each of the two sheriffs. The two full-dress coaches which were used had cost 225 guineas and the horses to pull them, £150. Convention has it that the lord mayor, his/her business and/or City livery company is responsible for underwriting the cost of their term of office. The position does come with a certain pecuniary allowance, but the majority must be met by the individual's resources. Around the time of Sydney's term of office, the allowance was some £10,000 with an additional £8,000 or more having to be found to make up the shortfall. The sums involved today are considerably higher!

However, the duties of the lord mayor were certainly not confined to being driven around in a gilt coach and giving dinners at the Mansion House or the Guildhall. There were, and still are, many and varied serious jobs which had to be woven into the mayoral schedule; even during Sydney's term the list was substantial. He had to preside over the sitting of the Court of Aldermen in their Court at the meeting of the Court of Common Council and at the Common Hall. He presided as judge of the Court of Hustings, was chief commissioner of the Central Criminal Court which he had to visit officially twice during each session and presided over the London Sessions held at the Guildhall. He was escheator-general in the City of London and Southwark, fortunately a job very rarely required. As chief conservator of the Thames he had to hold eight courts a year. There were daily sessions which involved signing copious affidavits to notarial documents required both at home and in the colonies. As the ex-officio chief of the Sewage Commissioners, he was required to attend committees of the municipal body and others. He was also required to be continually in correspondence with members of the government and presided at many, if not all, of the public meetings held in the City. Foreign dignitaries visiting London would always have an acknowledged claim on his time and hospitality and as an ex-officio member of the sovereign's Privy Council would have to attend its meeting on accession of a new king or queen, something which was obviously not necessary during Sydney's tenure.

If his time was not sufficiently occupied with the business of the City and Corporation and the other interests which naturally grew from it, there were other institutions — educational, charitable and religious — which would look to the lord mayor for official, if not personal, assistance. These would include a governor of Greenwich Hospital, King's College, Christ's Hospital, of St Bartholomew's and St Thomas' Hospitals. Along with the Archbishop of Canterbury and the Bishop of

London, a trustee of St Paul's Cathedral. Again, if that wasn't enough, the lord mayor was required to sit regularly in his own justice room at the Mansion House for at least three hours daily to administer the law.

Right up until the coronation of George IV in 1821 the lord mayor has acted as chief butler to the sovereign, receiving a gold cup as his fee. Even more recently than that the official household included other officers besides the sword-bearer, the macebearer and the marshal. These were the serjeant carvers, serjeants-of-chamber and his esquires; in his little kingdom of one square mile, the lord mayor is king.

By the time Sydney came to office he had become widely known and not just in the City of London. His fame had spread; the incidents of his career and his public services had given him celebrity status of an unusual kind, and people expected much from a man who had wrestled Dumfriesshire from the grip of the Duke of Buccleuch. It has sometimes been the sport of certain groups to belittle the office of lord mayor of London by saying that, generally, the holders of such a position were simply traders and nothing more. Outsiders, people from higher social positions and of certain intellectual capacities felt they were more inclined to leave the office to enriched shopkeepers whose views of life were formed behind a counter. This was possibly true, in some cases, but this type of comment was not something that gave Sydney any cause for concern.

In order to even be considered eligible for the office of the lord mayor a candidate was required to be master of their own particular City livery company. In Sydney's case this was the Worshipful Company of Stationers and Newspaper Makers whose Hall is situated a stone's throw from St Paul's Cathedral in Ave Maria Lane. At the time of Sydney's appointment, it was very unusual for a printer to become lord mayor and at the time of writing only eight past masters of the Stationers' Company have risen to that lofty position — two of them being Waterlows. There were also two distinctly different organisations who were also interested in the appointment and looked on it with some pleasure. One of these groups was the two thousand or so employees of Waterlow & Sons, the other being the tenants of the Improved Industrial Dwellings Company who owed him the possession of comfortable and sanitary rooms in which to live.

It would be safe to take for granted that Sydney discharged his official mayoral duties and functions as previously described with grace, good humour and thoroughness as, it is hoped, every holder of that office will do. However, what distinguishes one lord mayoralty from another is, firstly, the character of the person in question and the degree of intelligent energy which he or she brings to the conduct of their official life; the second is the use of the office for the promotion of schemes of the holder's own devising and execution which are not official or obligatory to the post. There were several of the latter during Sydney's year in office which bore the hallmarks of his effort and initiative.

'From the period when I first began to devote some time and attention to public questions, I have always held that the rights and liberties so largely enjoyed by the English nation were mainly owing to the development of municipal spirit throughout all the boroughs and cities in the kingdom. This love of municipal — or, rather, local — self-government was very much crushed and depressed by the passing of the Municipal Reform Act, which under the name of reform deprived the burgesses of the power of managing their own affairs which is essential to the life of a free community. Because the old Corporations were guilty of great jobbery, and by the perversion of the spirit of their charters, the new Corporations, when reformed, were placed in tutelage to the Local Government Board in London. I had for a long time felt that some attempt should be made to induce the Ministry to persuade Parliament to give all the municipalities greater power and control over the funds raised by themselves, and expended on public works in their own district, without compelling them to obtain the sanction of some officials in London before bringing any bill in Parliament to carry out their schemes.'

Admitting that many of the provincial corporations, especially the smaller ones, had abused their spending powers, Sydney offset their faults against the good workings of the Corporation of London.

'I think I am entitled to refer to the history of the Corporation of London as the best evidence of the advantages which a municipality may confer on the community by an honest, wise, and discreet exercise of an independent power over the funds.

'In centuries past the Corporation not only possessed a very large amount of real property, but have also been trustees for what was known as the Bridge House Estates. They have managed these estates with so much judgement that the revenues derived from them have increased enormously. The City of London is a county in itself, and the magistrates have hitherto never levied any rates on the citizens for county purposes, the expenses in this respect having been paid out of the City's cash. Although the Bridge House Estates were originally left for the purpose of being applied towards the cost of rebuilding London Bridge, the revenues, under the care of the Corporation, have been so well managed, and have so largely increased, that they have not only paid the cost of rebuilding London Bridge once, Blackfriars Bridge twice, and the noble bridge known as Holborn Viaduct, but they have recently been charged with the cost of building the beautiful bridge known as the Tower Bridge.

'I think we may fairly ask ourselves whether, if all these great public improvements had been compelled to be carried out under the management and control of a government department, such great benefits would have been secured to the public without imposing any taxation upon the citizens for the purpose.'

In the hope of giving effect to these views, Sydney resolved to invite all the mayors, Right Worshipful and Worshipful, to a banquet. This was almost certainly the first of its kind ever given in the City or elsewhere for that matter. The great event was held in the Egyptian Hall of the Mansion House, the lord mayor's official residence in the City. In all, two hundred mayors attended from all over the country, wearing their ermine-trimmed scarlet robes with lace ruffles and bedecked in their golden badges and chains of office. The Prime Minister, William Gladstone, also attended as did several ambassadors and foreign ministers from several countries with the French ambassador at their head.

During the lord mayor's toast for the evening of "prosperity to the Municipal Corporations of England and Wales", Sydney rather forcefully restated his views expressed above. He urged that every municipal body should have charge of all the affairs of its own city. If they do well, then they may feel justified in the confidence placed in them; if they do not, punish them. Whatever the eventual outcome they should be given the power and held accountable. However, he was quick to point out that these powers and proceedings must be kept public, the publicity being a guarantee of their honesty.

The prime minister then responded in a toast to Sydney:

'I ask you to drink the health of the lord mayor of London — in the first place because he is lord mayor of London, and that is a title sufficient to commend you to his esteem. But I ask you also to drink it on grounds which are more characteristic of himself. In times like these, it is much that we should be able to induce distinguished and able members of the metropolitan community to bear the burden of civic office. But what is even more important is that those whom the Almighty has blessed with prosperity and wealth should, when they have undertaken official responsibilities, still feel themselves animated by a sense of duty with regard to their poorer fellow creatures, and should engage, as the lord mayor has done, in works of humanity and beneficence. We are in these days too much inclined to indulge in the temptations to ease, arising from the growth of opulence amongst us; but never let us forget that, along with that growth, there is an ever-widening career for those who undertake the task of endeavouring to meet the necessities of their fellow creatures.

'And I believe I may truly say that no one in this great community has earned a more just title to the admiration and respect of his fellow citizens than the lord mayor has in connection with such works as I have mentioned.'

Despite the eventual future increase of power of the Local Government Board over local legislatures, there

113

was one objective that Sydney's words were able to achieve. He had stirred the spirit of local independence in the civic consciousness. First Southampton, then Liverpool, Manchester and York took up the strain. The mayor and Corporation of Southampton asked the lord mayor of London, accompanied by the two sheriffs, Sir Thomas White and Sir Frederick Perkins, to attend a banquet to help with strengthening public opinion in favour of the granting of fuller control for municipalities over their own affairs, and the right to be able to spend money in their own way. The banquet proved to be a resounding success in achieving its aim.

Slowly but surely a movement began to gather momentum. A meeting was convened in London in early 1873 in connection with the Municipal Corporations Association at which a large number of the chief magistrates from all over the country were present. The whole association was organised on a working basis and a resolution was adopted to hold another banquet with the lord mayor of London as the chief guest and the mayors of cities and boroughs in England to be the hosts. York was chosen as the location for this event, partially because of its beautiful Guildhall, a notable example of Gothic architecture of the period; originally built in 1446 by the mayor, commonalty and the master and brethren of the Guild of St Christopher during the reign of Henry VI.

The banquet became a pageant; the lord mayor and sheriffs of London travelled up in their robes of state and were met at the station by the lord mayor, aldermen, town council and city officers of York. The station itself was covered in sumptuous crimson carpeting and turned into an amphitheatre for the seated spectators. The procession ended up being a mile long with the lord mayor of London arriving in full state. Noblemen had travelled in from the countryside to witness the event and the people of York cheered at the spectacle.

Obviously, there was something more than a dispute between the municipalities and the Local Government Board about the supervision of expenditure and cost of the event. Sydney's reaction was predictable:

'My original object was to cement still more closely that bond of union and good understanding which ought to exist between municipalities for the purpose of maintaining free and unfettered local self-government in antagonism to the principal of centralisation. The municipal corporations of our country are constantly increasing in power and are no mean safeguards to the preservation of the civil and religious liberty which we enjoy.'

He later said at the banquet held at York:

'Our municipal institutions represented in an especial way the principal of self-government and differed materially from all other forms of local administration. They were not only administrative, but also legislative, and embodied that most essential principal of self-government, the right of administering justice by the representatives of the people, and in their name.'

Every time Sydney touched on this subject it was easy to see that his mind was saturated with the ideas which had originally been the foundations of English liberty and which remain so today.

In July 1873 the baronetcy of *Waterlow of London* was conferred on Sydney and officially announced in the *London Gazette*:

'Whitehall — July 29, 1873.

'The Queen has been pleased to direct letters patent to be framed under the Great Seal granting the dignity of a baronet of the United Kingdom of Great Britain and Ireland unto the Right Honourable Sir Sydney Hedley Waterlow, of Fairseat, in the parish of Wrotham, the County of Kent, and of Highgate, the County of Middlesex, Knight, Lord Mayor of the City of London, and the heirs of his body lawfully begotten.'

After making the announcement, William Gladstone was quick to add his comment on the conferral:

'I cannot convey to your Lordship the tender of this honour without adding what lively satisfaction I feel in making it to one who, independently of the high office which he holds, has deserved so well of the people of this great metropolis for an intelligent and indefatigable philanthropy.'

The creation was popular with all, even including those who did not look favourably on the Corporation of London and its dignities and dignitaries. Among the congratulations received by Sydney, none seemed to please him more than an address from the scholars of St Saviour's School where he had once been a scholar himself:

'It is the privilege of those who attain to distinguished positions in later life to serve as beacons to those who are only as yet entering upon its duties and labours, and your name has long been recorded by us as one whose examples we should follow, not only as a man of mark among old St Saviour's boys, but as one who, by his honourable career and unfailing energy in business, his deep interest in the welfare of the poor, and steady support of all measures for the spread of education, has obtained a position of commanding influence with this great community.'

In April 1873 the Lord Chamberlain officially announced the visit of the Shah of Persia to the City. The news was conveyed to the Court of Common Council who unanimously agreed that the Corporation should send an invitation to the shah to a reception at the Guildhall. It was also agreed to present their special guest with an address in Persian, his native tongue, given in the Persian spirit and sentiment:

'In the effulgent presence of His Most Holy Imperial Majesty, the King of Kings of the World and the Age, the Sultan, son of Sultan, son of a Sultan, Nasred Deen Shah — may God preserve his kingdom for ever.

'We, the lord mayor and people on whom devolved the government of the City of London, sincerely approaching his angel-guarded threshold, with our hands on our breasts and standing in the appointed place on the feet of supplication, present this petition.'

Fanciful stuff!

While I am certain that Sydney would have wished to be remembered for other works during his term of office rather than his hospitality, he did give one dinner in the Egyptian Hall at the Mansion House on Christmas Day 1872 for which there cannot have been many precedents set. It was a family dinner and both he and his wife's families were very numerous. The party included Sydney's father, James, his own and his wife's brothers and sisters, their children and grandchildren, uncles and aunts, nephews and nieces. In all, two hundred people were invited of whom one hundred and eighty were present; seventeen of those were of a young enough age as to have need of their nurses. At the dinner, James Waterlow, now eighty-three years of age, had around him four sons, three daughters, two sons-in-law, four daughters-in-law, forty-nine grandchildren and fourteen great-grandchildren. There was a baron of beef weighing in at 276lbs which had to be carried into the Hall by four men; this was followed by a huge plum pudding of 117lbs garnished with holly and blazing spirit. The only toast was to the health of Sydney's father who also made the only speech which included the sentiment that:

'the next best thing to being lord mayor was to be the lord mayor's father.'

He must have felt a proud man indeed.

Even more important than the traditions of hospitality which the lord mayor is renowned for are the episodes of charitable works sanctioned by the incumbent, and Sydney was no different than his predecessors nor those who came after him. Examples of events during Sydney's time included the disaster of the ship *Northfleet*. This was sunk by a steamer in the English Channel which then failed to stop and aid the stricken vessel. This resulted in the death of three-quarters of the four hundred souls on board including the captain and all his officers. After a meeting at the Mansion House a subscription of £8,000 was made towards the disaster fund; the City charities were not only confined to necessities within domestic shores. In November 1872 there were huge floods in Ferrara and other parts of northern Italy which destroyed large amounts of property and left many people homeless and destitute. The Mansion House made it known that it was co-ordinating a relief fund to aid in the disaster recovery and, as well as many donations from the population, this also prompted a cheque for £400 from the queen and the Corporation donated 500 guineas. As the money came in it was immediately dispatched to the Minister of Foreign Affairs in Rome. In all some £7,300 was sent with the Italian government being quick to show their gratitude to the queen, the City and the population of the country. The King of Italy "to mark the high estimation in which His Majesty held the powerful, cordial, and personal support of the lord mayor", conferred on Sydney the distinction of Commander of the Order of the Crown of Italy. The Chevalier Cadorna, Italian Ambassador in London, wrote:

'No one knows better than I how this distinction will be worthily and justly placed, and it is with a feeling of real pleasure that I have the honour to make known to you the king's intention.'

Sydney accepted the order with his customary humility and good grace.

To increase his opportunities of charitable usefulness, the new lord mayor became a life governor of a great number of the charitable institutions of the metropolis. He then set about attempting to abolish the system under which each subscriber to a charity is entitled to votes for beneficiaries in proportion to the amount of the subscription. It was a system which encouraged abuse and where money ended up being wasted. Sydney convened a meeting at the Mansion House; William Gladstone, unable to attend, sent along a letter of support as did Lord Shaftesbury. Florence Nightingale described the system as "the best system for electing the least eligible", adding: "There is a traffic in votes; it is a scheme to gratify gambling propensities", backing up her words by declaring that she had withdrawn her support from every institution which dealt in this practice. The press, with the exception of one newspaper, also raised their collective voice in support.

The ensuing meeting in the Egyptian Hall was packed with secretaries, managers, paid officials, clerks and their friends, by all the agents and organisers of electioneering and all those profiting by the existing method. They would not allow the lord mayor to be heard or listen to the likes of the Marquis of Westminster and Mr Samuel Morley and they carried a vote with a very large majority to keep the situation as it existed. While this was the result that Sydney had not foreseen, he was, nevertheless, un-phased by the result, and, in reply, founded the Charity Voting Reform Association. This eventually managed to influence several charities to abolish the system while others were forced to reform some of the worst practices. As a result of this, since 1873 no new charity has set up a proxy voting system.

The next project on the list was the dealing with the question of the schools in the City. Two years previously a plan for remodelling the existing schools had been matured by Sydney and the Rev. William Rogers, an informed City authority on the subject. At the time, the schools were barely more than charitable institutions. It was now proposed to leave the larger and wealthier schools to continue unaltered and to amalgamate the others with the income from the invested funds being used to create three schools of one thousand children in each. Unsurprisingly, there was opposition to the plan with the groups involved in the abusing of the system being the most vocal against the reform. Again, a meeting was held in the Egyptian Hall at the Mansion House and, again, Sydney was voted down and his proposals rejected.

'I was disappointed with the result but not disheartened. Experience has taught me that those who seek to carry out reforms in ancient institutions, in order to place them in thorough harmony with the public opinion of the time, must not expect to succeed in their first or even second attempt.'

Even during Sydney's term of office, a lot of the old City customs were starting to disappear as he recalled:

'In the month of December 1872, I received from the Horse Guards a memorandum giving me the password to the Tower for every day in the months of January, February, and March; and similar lists were forwarded quarterly to enable me, as chief magistrate of the City of London, to pass the Guards at the Tower. These lists were signed by Her Majesty's own hand, being marked, "Approved — Victoria R." They have, I believe, been long since discontinued. They were a remnant of the old right which belonged to the lord mayor of London, of refusing admittance to the queen's troops within the City walls, and gave the lord mayor the right, as head of the trained bands of the City of London, to pass within the precincts of the Tower.

'At this time, it was also the practice of the War Office authorities, whenever they wished to pass queen's troops through the City, to obtain previously from the lord mayor an order permitting their entry within the City walls.'

Sydney, like all aldermen, was an ex-officio member of Queen Anne's Bounty Board, sitting in Dean's Yard, Westminster. As a result of this he found himself in contact with bishops and other high-ranking officials of a church to which he did not belong. Nevertheless, they welcomed him as a man well used to dealing with land and property; dilapidations of rectories and vicarages, charges upon the estates of deceased incumbents, sums to be fixed by new incumbents for repairs and other issues often came before the board. Sydney was more than happy to provide both a layman's and businessman's opinion. He often pushed to reduce the legal fees which came as an unwanted burden on new incumbents, often men without any private income. The solicitors' fees were particularly heavy in some cases and Sydney had more than one contest with Samuel Wilberforce, the then Bishop of Winchester, concerning the matter. It turned out that the private solicitor and the solicitor to the board were, in fact, one and the same; the bishop, thinking more of his legal friend's interest than that of the clergy, used his authority to maintain the legal fees payable. Some of the younger bishops also took exception to this and, with help from Sydney and other members of the board, succeeded in reducing the fees. In this instance it appeared that a Unitarian layman had been a better friend to the Church than one of its own bishops.

There are many other instances, while not so remarkable in their own right, also serve to illustrate the multifarious nature of Sydney's duties as well as his own personal energy. In 1869 an Act of Parliament had been passed for the freeing of the toll-bridges over the River Thames between Staines and the Tower of London. Sydney was on the commission for this and Kew Bridge, the last of these, was not freed until his time in office as lord mayor, but at a cost of £57,300. However, the liberation ceremony was such that it left no doubt in the minds of the public what was taking place. The commission was summoned to meet at the Middlesex end of the bridge with Sydney at their head, and, with the help of a few navvies, the toll gate was removed from its hinges. With the commissioners following in procession, the gate was then carried above the navvies' heads to the middle of the bridge and thrown into the river to the great cheers of everyone on both banks. No more tolls were levied for crossing Kew Bridge.

Among some of the other more notable novelties of his time in office, on 29 March 1873 Sydney also gave "a dinner which had never been given by any previous lord mayor and has never been given since" in the Egyptian Hall to the Oxford and Cambridge Boat Race crews. There was a total of 174 guests in attendance equally distributed between the two universities. It seems as if the state and solemnity of an official banquet at the Mansion House was soon forgotten and both the two crews and their friends were united in an easy fellowship. With the advertised finishing time of midnight fast approaching nobody seemed anxious to leave; however, Sunday was respected in the City and they were eventually persuaded to depart. Although students, being students, took with them the main door key by way of protest which they also promptly returned in the morning. Sydney, proposing a toast to Cambridge, the winning crew, gave a small speech into which he put his whole soul into a subject which was altogether new to him, extolling the virtues of rowing and exercise which "stirs the Viking blood which runs in our veins", also stating that "outdoor life and sports are the best features of our modern civilisation".

Eventually Sydney's year of office drew to an end. On the day of the election of his successor, the rector of St Botolph, Bishopsgate, the Rev. William Rogers, preached a sermon at St Lawrence Jewry in front of the outgoing lord mayor and his successor, Mr Alderman Lusk, and other aldermen and officers of the Corporation.

'He [Sydney] has had great opportunities, and he has embraced those opportunities with energy and intelligence; he has filled the post with honour and has added dignity to the office by his liberality, by his open-handed hospitality, and by his impartial administration of justice. Many difficult questions have come before him for judgement, and he has pronounced sentence with equity and discretion, commending himself to the approval of his fellow citizens.'

The Court of Aldermen were also quick to pass a resolution of thanks to the retiring lord mayor:

'That the cordial thanks of this Court are due, and are hereby given, to the Right Hon. Sir Sydney Hedley Waterlow, Bart., late Lord Mayor of this City, for the dignity, efficiency, and zeal with which he has discharged the many and important duties of Chief Magistrate during the past year; for the assiduity and impartiality with which he has performed his official functions; for the energetic course pursued by him in the maintenance and support of municipal institutions; for his exertions in the cause of charity, his liberal hospitality, his courtesy and accessibility whenever waited upon for assistance and advice; and for the manner in which he has uniformly upheld the dignity and privileges of the City of London and the interests and rights of his fellow citizens.'

It was always Sydney's wish to "leave the ancient and honourable office as unsullied and free from stain as when he accepted it". He also said of himself:

'I have never used the great power and influence of my office for the purpose of gratifying my own personal feelings or of improving my own position pecuniarily. As in the case of most lord mayors, overtures were constantly made to me to join lucrative commercial and industrial companies, but my answer was invariably the same to all; namely, that during my mayoralty I could not listen to offers of that kind. From the first I made up my mind that my conduct in that respect must be above suspicion. I spared neither time, labour, nor expense, in endeavouring to sustain the dignity of the office.'

Despite all the official recognition and respect of Sydney's time in office, there is also one incident to be related to illustrate that the life of a lord mayor is not always as glamorous as sometimes perceived. Although the lord mayor's official residence is the Mansion House in the City, during his term of office Sydney continued to travel to and from his home at the top of Highgate Hill to work every day, riding in a horse-drawn carriage provided by the Corporation. Consequently, as a private citizen, he was just as vulnerable to everyday inconveniences as reported in *The Times* of 20 November 1872:

'ROBBING THE LORD MAYOR — Fairseat House, Highgate, the private residence of the lord mayor, was broken into on Monday evening. The thieves entered the house between seven and eight o'clock, while the whole family were at dinner and most of the servants engaged.

'They seem to have procured a short ladder from a hay rick in the grounds, and with this they reached the window of the lady mayoress. They there forced open several drawers and cupboards and stole many articles of jewellery of the value of about £300. The robbery was not discovered, till some time later in the evening, but the thieves had then managed to escape.

'Among the articles said to have been stolen are the insignia of the Order of the Medjidic, conferred upon the lord mayor by the Sultan on his visit to the City, some Corporation medals and badges, and, what was a great deal more prized by the family, some jewellery which had belonged to his Lordship's eldest son [Frank], who died last year. The matter has been placed in the hands of the police.'

Unfortunately, there does not appear to be any further reports on the progress of the official investigation into the matter and the stolen items were never recovered.

Working as a compositor in Paris, 1844

Lord Mayor of London, 1872

The new Lord Mayor – *Vanity Fair*, November 1872

Anna Maria, Sydney's first wife

Bust of Sydney at Bart's Hospital
courtesy of Bart's Health NHS Trust Archives

Annual meeting of the Hospital Sunday Fund at the
Mansion House, 1895

Trosley Towers exterior

Trosley Towers entrance hall

Sydney and Margaret in the grounds at Trosley, c.1904

Sydney with daughter Ruth (sitting), granddaughter
Muriel, and great-grandchildren Frank and Harold,
c.1903
with kind permission of Ruth Shepley

Sydney's statue, Waterlow Park

Sydney's statue, Westminster School, Victoria

Sydney's gravestone before installation

Sydney's gravestone today

Waterlow of London coat of arms hanging in
Stationers' Hall

Sir Sydney Hedley Waterlow, Bt. KCVO
1822 - 1906

CHAPTER IX
THE IRISH SOCIETY

By the time he had reached the age of fifty and was fortunate enough to be reaping the rewards of his enterprises, Sydney found that tasks and duties were being heaped upon him more than ever. He was not a man who ever apportioned time for well-earned leisure, and he was certainly not a man who would sum up his philosophy of life in a single sentence. The hard work which he had had to endure during the early years of his life had done nothing except increase his appetite for more of the same. One such of these many endeavours was the governorship of the Irish Society; this position had become vacant during the summer months of 1873, towards the latter part of his term as lord mayor, when alderman Sir William Rose was forced to resign from the position due to ill health. Owing to the respect that Sydney already commanded, it took the Court of Common Council no time at all to choose Sydney as Rose's successor and he remained the society's governor until the autumn of 1883.

So why did there need to be an Irish Society in London and what was it that tempted Sydney to want to become its governor?

The Honourable the Irish Society, to give it its proper name, was set up in 1613 after the incorporation of a Royal Charter by James I as a consortium of livery companies of the City of London during the Plantation of Ulster. In its first few decades of existence, it rebuilt the city of Derry and the town of Coleraine and for centuries it owned property and fishing rights near both towns. Some of the society's profits were used to develop the economy and infrastructure of the area while some was also returned to the London investors and a portion of it being used for charitable work. There is no doubt that it was the, by now, mainly charitable work performed by the society which attracted Sydney to the task ahead and he began to approach the project with all his usual fervour.

Sydney visited his new 'dominions' in August 1873 and immediately set about looking into the question of schools, the granting of leases, the Presbyterian Institute, the building of a new town hall, of fisheries, ferries and many other matters. He took nothing for granted and personally made substantial enquires into every matter. In Coleraine he was pleased to find the schools that had been built and maintained by the society, flourishing and educating nearly five hundred pupils, and pledged that he would do everything in his power to ensure the society continued to maintain the high standards he had witnessed. In a few instances, notably in the case of the Presbyterian Institute, some good opportunities for improvement had not been taken advantage of and Sydney reminded them that the society would only help those who helped themselves. The new governor spent two weeks conducting this tour, continuing to do so every year, inspecting the condition and progress of the estates, his recommendations being based on justice tempered with kindness, being mindful of all interests.

Even a few ecclesiastical problems were resolved. In Derry, there was one educational establishment called Foyle College which, although having room for sixty pupils to board, in fact only had four students doing so. The reason for its unpopularity was due to it being an ecclesiastical establishment, being a diocesan church school. The headmaster was required to be a member of the Episcopal Church of Ireland and the boys all had to attend daily Episcopal service which was not popular with the Presbyterians. Sydney conducted a meeting with the Bishop of Derry, Dr Alexander, a large-minded man with a build to match. In the meeting, the bishop proposed a new governing body which should not include any Episcopal or sectarian members. The proposal was then taken to Parliament by Sydney where he introduced a new bill to set up the new governing body for Foyle College and that it should consist of five ex-officio members: the Bishop of Derry, the Governor and Deputy-Governor of the Irish Society, the Mayor of Derry and the Moderator of the General Assembly. Under this proposal the bishop would represent the Church, and the moderator would speak for the Presbyterians, leaving the three other governors as neutrals and in the majority. The bill was passed in 1874 and such was its success that no more trouble was encountered. Under the Act and under the guidance of the new headmaster, the previously only four students rapidly became sixty and the college was filled to capacity.

With an eye open to politics and to Prime Minister Gladstone's mind, Sydney, as governor, very concerned with the value of the Irish Society's property as well as with his duties, came to the belief that this property in the county of Londonderry would soon decrease in value. His own livery company, the Stationers', although having no interest of its own, pecuniary or otherwise, found itself holding part of the share granted to the Skinners' Company. In Sydney's words:

'As the Skinners were willing to treat for the purchase of the Stationers' share, I took an active part in negotiating the sale, and was able to induce the Skinners' Company to give £40,000 for the purchase of the Stationers' share. This was in 1875. The changes which took place in the Land Laws in Ireland during the ensuing fifteen years reduced the value of the land to half the price which was then obtained.'

It was unfortunate that during the following two years after this transaction Sydney was to meet a parliamentary attack on the society. Charles Lewis, Member of Parliament for Derry, put forward a motion that a Parliamentary Select Committee should hold an enquiry into the constitution, management and annual expenditure of the society and how it could potentially be re-organised and improved. However, as Sydney was due to be abroad at the time of the committee's meeting, Lewis was happy to postpone the motion until the following year. It was also discovered that a royal commission had already reported on the society as far back as 1853 and had recommended that the society be dissolved, its charter repealed, and its property handed over to a new set of trustees.

In presenting his motion, armed with all this newfound information, Lewis was quietly confident that he would gather some strong support. However, rather than gaining support for his cause, the only petitions received were strongly against the motion. Despite obtaining the accounts for the years 1865 to 1874 which showed several discrepancies, the arguments put forward in the society's defence by Sydney, Sir William McArthur (Irish businessman and Liberal politician) and Sir J. C. Lawrence (alderman and Liberal politician) were so convincing that Lewis had no other option but to withdraw his motion. So persuasive were the defence arguments that the House even expressed a concern to re-enforce their approval of Sydney as governor of the society. To dispel the notion that the society existed purely for profitable gains, Sydney briefly mentioned some of the benefits it had bestowed. The bridge over the River Foyle was a toll bridge. On one side were the great factories; on the other, the poorer districts where the workmen lived. In order to alleviate the burden of the toll for the workers, he offered, subject to his colleagues' approval, £40,000 towards paying off the bridge debt of £80,000 if the people could levy a rate to pay for the other half. This was greeted with cheers; the rate was levied, and the toll bridge was made free. The society also donated a grant of some £40,000 to improve the navigation of the River Bann; they gave a site for a new market for Coleraine aptly named the Waterlow Market. However, Sydney was also keen to point out that while these improvements were recent, the benefactions of the society began some two hundred years previously.

'Those who have visited the cathedral at Londonderry must have noticed an old black stone in the porch, upon which certain letters have been rudely carved in years long gone by. They run thus:

"If stones could speak, they London's praise would sound,

That built this church from out the ground".

'But I venture to think that, if stones could speak, the stones in almost every church and day school in Londonderry and Coleraine, in which the Protestant religion has been taught these last two centuries, would chant the same song; and not only of every church and every school, but the stones of the manses attached to those churches, and the stones of the fortifications by which the town is surrounded, would be equally anxious

143

to offer their share of praise to the Irish Society and the Corporation of the City of London.'

London and its livery companies not only built the walls which saved the city of Londonderry when under siege, they also came to its defence with guns and supplies. Even today the city's ramparts display cannon bearing the names of their donors, Vintners', Fishmongers', Merchant Taylors', Grocers' and Mercers' Companies, and several on which the arms of the Irish Society are still visible. At the cessation of hostilities, the society also spent large sums of money rebuilding the city. The outcome of this work became the principal reason why the old town of Derry changed its name to Londonderry in recognition of London's services during this time.

On Sydney's ninth re-election in 1881 he thanked the Common Council for his re-election and referred to the governorship as a position of great responsibility but one not un-mixed with a certain anxiety.

'And never, perhaps, more than the present time, when from one end of Ireland to the other, but more especially in the Centre, the South, and the South-West, the tenant-farmers have been induced by selfish and designing men to set themselves in opposition to their landlords, and to repudiate their legal obligations, and to refuse to pay any rent except such terms as they may consider to be fair and reasonable. The agents of the Land League have, up to the present, done very little harm in the districts in which the estates of the Irish

Society are situated. I venture to think that this arises from the fair and generous policy which has guided the society in dealing with the tenants, and from the kindly feeling that has for some years past existed between the Irish Society and the inhabitants generally of Londonderry and Coleraine.'

Sydney goes on to say that during the whole period of his governorship there was not one case of eviction. There was one occasion that a notice of eviction was served but that the Land Court had decided that the increase in rent was fair and the tenant was happy to accept the finding of the court and paid up.

'The society have always endeavoured to give to their agricultural tenants fixity of tenure, fair rents, and freedom of sale, subject only to the condition that any intending purchaser shall have fair notice of the time when the farms may have to be revalued. I venture to think no tenant should ask more, and no landlord should give less, especially in cases where the tenants have made permanent improvements on the farm.'

Two years later, in the autumn of 1883, Sydney resigned as governor after eleven years of continuous service. He had administered the estates of the Irish Society with prudence and equality; he had left Londonderry and Coleraine, as far as their prosperity was concerned in the eyes of the society, better and more prosperous than he had found them. He had restored good relations when things had gone wrong and had won the confidence of those concerned.

Free bridges, better schools, a contented and thriving tenantry, improved buildings and a more business-like administration were among the results of his work. He had had to endure opposition from all sides, his fellow Members of Parliament, Irish leaders who preached hatred of England as the first duty of every true Irishman; through it all he had won the confidence of the tenants of the society. The answer was simple; he was a strong-willed and just man who considered the advantages of the society and the community it serviced to be inextricably entwined, one acting as an advantage to the other.

The society remains in existence today as a 'relatively small grant-giving charitable body' — a shadow of its former self. Its educational grants are funded by its remaining property, including the Walls of Derry, a tourist attraction and heritage site, and fisheries on the River Bann. It is still based in London, with a 'representative' resident in County Londonderry. It continues to remain closely linked with the City of London, with its governor traditionally being a former lord mayor of London and members of the Court of Aldermen and Court of Common Council of the Corporation of London constituting members of the Court of the Honourable the Irish Society.

CHAPTER X
ROYAL COMMISSIONS

There was a time when the government of the day was in the habit of calling upon the country's busiest men to perform unpaid service on its many royal commissions; unsurprisingly, Sydney was one of those prevailed upon on a frequent basis. One of the first occasions was in 1870 when the Home Secretary, Henry Bruce, invited him to act on the commission to enquire into friendly societies and benefit societies. The request came in the form of a letter from Bruce, using all his most charming powers of persuasion:

'The lively interest you have taken in all that concerns the working classes, and your successful exertions on their behalf, would render your acceptance as gratifying to them as it would be to me.'

Once fully appointed, the commission proved to be a strong one, with the noted statesman, Sir Stafford Northcote as chairman. There was in existence, at that time, in excess of thirty-two thousand benefit and friendly societies with over four million members, as well as another four million who had an interest in their prosperity, namely the wives and children of the members. The accumulated funds of these societies amounted to in excess of £11,000,000, their aggregate incomes estimated at £5,000,000 and some of those were more than a century old. The commission met first in London and then in major centres throughout England, Ireland and Scotland. The enquiries continued until March 1874 when a final report was presented to the House of Commons.

Owing to the thoroughness of the commission's work the results were used as a basis for a new piece of legislation. A bill was introduced and passed through Parliament with the object of better protecting those people who had invested their money in the societies.

Prior to this, in 1867, Sydney had been a somewhat surprising inclusion in the Judicature Commission which had been appointed to enquire into the constitution of the High Court of Chancery, the Superior Courts of Common Law, the Central Criminal Court, the Probate and Divorce Court and the Courts of Common Pleas. The commission was also tasked to investigate "all other matters relating to the administration of justice". This commission, as expected, was heavily weighted in favour of members of the legal profession; headed up by the Lord Chancellor, supported by ex-Lord Chancellors, the Lord Chief Justice and other experienced judges. In order to maintain a modicum of balance it also included Members of Parliament and people from other walks of life outside the justice system.

This commission lasted for five years, with Sydney's first effort being to induce the judges to give up the 'circuit' system. He was of the opinion that it inflicted injury and loss upon metropolitan suitors, as the judges often had to lay aside important business in London in order to try a few lesser, unimportant cases in provincial towns and cities. However, the judges did not accede to Sydney's point of view, there was nothing that could persuade them otherwise and they were clearly not to be influenced by those outside the legal system.

As the years went by and more evidence was heard, the government decided to enlarge the original remit of the commission and added the question of setting up tribunals of commerce. This was something about which Sydney knew a considerable amount; he had accumulated the commercial experience to be able to understand the workings of this question and he wasted no time in putting the view of the City to the judges and other lawyers. Unsurprisingly, this fell on deaf ears and, in protest, Sydney refused to sign the third report, setting out his objections in a memorandum:

'I am unable to agree with all the recommendations of this report, and therefore do not sign it. I feel very strongly that, in a great commercial country like England, tribunals can and ought to be established where suitors might obtain a decision on their differences more promptly, and much less expensively, than in the Superior Courts as at present constituted and regulated.

'Those who support the present system of trying mercantile disputes seem to regard them all as hostile litigation, and lose sight of the fact that, in the majority of cases where differences arise between merchants or traders, both parties would rejoice to obtain a prompt settlement by a legal tribunal duly constituted, and to continue their friendly commercial relations. The present system too frequently works a denial of justice, or inflicts on the suitor a long-pending, worrying lawsuit, the solicitors on either side pleading in their clients' interest every technical point, and thus engendering a bitterness which destroys all future confidence and puts an end to further mercantile dealings.

'It is essential that the procedure of our Mercantile Courts (whether called Tribunals of Commerce or by any other name) should be of the simplest and most summary character, similar to that of the Tribunals of Commerce in Hamburg or in France, or before justices of the peace in this country, as recommended by the Select Committee of the House of Commons in 1871.

'The liberty of the subject is, perhaps, more jealously guarded in this country than property. If the summary jurisdiction conferred on justices of the peace in criminal cases, when exercised by gentlemen who are not lawyers, gives satisfaction, it can scarcely be doubted that a similar jurisdiction in civil cases would be equally acceptable.'

But it was not to be. There was a strong belief in the world of commerce and general business that such tribunals would be of great use, but neither the belief nor the examples of Paris and Hamburg were able to sway the legal minds.

In 1880, towards the end of the new session of Parliament under Gladstone's government, the prime minister was persuaded to appoint a royal commission of enquiry into the City livery companies, this being popular subject of debate among the more radically minded, much as it is today. The royal warrant was dated 29 July 1880 and the commission was formed of as strongly a conservative group of members as could be expected. The Earl of Derby, the Duke of Bedford, Viscount Sherbrooke, Lord Coleridge, Sir Richard Cross (later Viscount Cross), Sir Nathan Mayer Rothschild (later Lord Rothschild), Sir William James Cotton MP, Thomas Burt (Parliamentary Secretary to the Board of Trade) and Sydney himself. It was intended to be a commission that commanded confidence, there was no man on it who was not more than qualified to be a member. Naturally, Sydney was very much on home ground, knowing his subject inside out. Up to that point he had direct interest in the whole business as a member of the livery companies, ex-master of Stationers' Company, and, for nearly twenty years, very closely associated with City affairs and with the government of the City of London.

The remit of the commission was far reaching; the commissioners were directed to enquire into the constitution and powers of several of the livery companies, and into all circumstances connected with their property holdings and into the uses to which their income was applied. Taking the top twelve livery companies at that time, their aggregate income in the year of the appointment of the commission was in the region of £800,000 (£67,000,000 in 2020), of which, £200,000 (£16,800,000) was trust income. The rateable value of the Halls was approximately £35,000 (£2,940,000), schools and alms houses about £15,000 (£1,260,000), and plate and furniture not less than £50,000 (£4,200,000). Evidence received by the commission showed that the companies' estates were regularly and rapidly increasing in value and at that time were reckoned to be in the region of £15,000,000 (£1.26 billion) which was estimated to rise to approximately £25,000,000 (£2.1 billion) within twenty-five years.

Sydney believed it was virtually impossible to determine when the livery companies or the ancient guilds of London came into being. Some of them were almost certainly in existence even before the Norman Conquest, and it was through them that the independence of London was won and established. The musician and author Reuben Hallam (1818-1908) described them as "fraternities by voluntary compact to relieve each other in poverty and protect each other from injury. Two essential characteristics belonged to them: the common banquet and the common purse. They readily became connected with the exercise of trades and with the training of apprentices."

As a member of two companies himself, Sydney was, unsurprisingly, very knowledgeable in the history and condition of the livery 'system'. His first, the Stationers', had seen him serve a seven-year apprenticeship in the printing trade; the first £100 that he had after receiving his Freedom was spent in taking up his livery with the company. He was called upon the Court in 1863, and for many years was the youngest member of its governing body. His admission to the Clothworkers' Company involved a compliment of an unusual kind. He was entered as a freeman, liveryman, a member of the Court and a past master, all in the same day! There appears to have been no precedent for this, as regular process ensures that it takes many years to get to that stage.

Generally, the livery companies came out of the enquiry relatively unscathed and in much better health than the 'radicals' had hoped. The commission had sat weekly for a year; witnesses came forward freely and it was clearly proved that the trust income of all the companies was carefully and honestly administered, in most cases without charge. It was further proved that in the case of the best-governed companies, one third of the corporate income was assigned to a charity of educational purpose. There were occasions when a few irregularities were discovered, but there was nothing so bad as for anyone to call for the abolition of the companies themselves. It was not so much a case of what had been done but rather what had not which laid them open to criticism suggesting the need for reforms. However, when it came to the presentation of the report and its recommendations, the commissioners were far from unanimous. Three members — Cross, Rothschild and Cotton — withheld their signatures from the following:

1. The companies should be prevented by Parliament from alienating their property.

2. They should publish their accounts annually, both corporate and trust.

3. Admission to the livery of a company should no longer carry with it the parliamentary franchise for London.

4. Each company to allocate one-third of its corporate income to purposes of admitted utility.

5. As the companies never die, they should pay annually a sum of money in commutation of succession duty.

Out of the five, all but one, the fifth, became law for which Sydney was responsible. It is embodied in the Act of Parliament which levies this tax on all corporations holding property in a similar way.

Naturally, Sydney had his views on the outcome:

'I cannot refer to the work of the Livery Companies Commission without calling attention to the admirable manner in which the companies initiated the work of technical education in this country. The first grant of £3,000 a year was voted on my motion by the Clothworkers' Company in 1876, after many discussions on the subject, commencing in 1870. In 1877 and in subsequent years the Drapers' and Goldsmiths', and nearly all the other large companies, formed an association for promoting the work. This association erected the college in Exhibition Road at a cost of more than £100,000, and it has for many years subscribed £25,000 to £40,000 per annum in promoting this national work all over the country.'

It was clear that some type of reform had been needed but more from within the companies themselves looking inward rather than from any external pressure.

CHAPTER XI
BART'S HOSPITAL

To this point, Sydney's life had been wholly concerned with directing his energies in the pursuit of some practical or useful project beneficial to his 'fellow-men', to use his own terminology; he was very much a captain of both industry and charity. Sydney was of a kind who imposed duties and obligations upon himself purely for the welfare of others, and none was more pertinent to this than the work he undertook for St Bartholomew's Hospital for over thirty years.

Despite a generation having passed since Sydney was apprenticed to a printer, he had never forgotten his early wish to become a doctor; medical and surgical matters still held an attraction for him. So, when, in 1863, his election to alderman made him an ex-officio governor of Bart's, St Thomas' and Bridewell Hospitals he seized on the opportunity to gain more of an insight into hospital workings. Initially he would only attend quarterly meetings but soon managed to find himself a place on the weekly committees.

Bart's Hospital is as much a part of London as Trafalgar Square or Tower Bridge. It stands in Smithfield on the north side of the Thames and was founded in 1123 by a man named Rahere, who was sometime jester and minstrel to Henry I. He is also recorded as being a canon of St Paul's Cathedral in 1115, when on a pilgrimage to Rome he fell ill and reputedly had a vision of St Bartholomew, who directed him to establish a religious hospital. Upon his return to England, he followed this calling and founded a priory at Smithfield in London, being installed as its prior, a position he held until his death.

The hospital received fresh charters in 1544 and 1547, and the first physician to accurately describe and document the blood circulation system of the human body, William Harvey, became the physician in charge of the hospital in October 1609. Escaping the Great Fire of 1666, the hospital was rebuilt in 1729. When Sydney started to take an interest, the establishment boasted 678 beds with room for seventy-five more in a convalescent home at Swanley, Kent. In addition, a further 150,000 outpatients were treated annually, and the attached medical school boasted some four hundred students.

Once again, Sydney found himself serving another type of apprenticeship to Bart's, as he did not become its treasurer until 1874. Prior to that, early in 1870, he had been appointed a member of the Central London Sick Asylum District Board, and in May he became chairman. This board was responsible for the care of the sick poor in the Central Metropolitan District who could not be treated properly in the workhouses. Obviously, this system no longer exists, but at the time it had control of several large hospitals and infirmaries. During Sydney's chairmanship an infirmary of 525 beds was built in Highgate under his supervision and close to his own house. The cost worked out at £110 per bed as opposed to £1,000 per bed at St Thomas' Hospital. The days of trained nurses in hospitals were only just dawning and St Thomas' Hospital in particular already had a training school which had been established by a certain Florence Nightingale. This formidable lady came readily to Sydney's aid with help for the Highgate Infirmary, and it was largely due to her that it was supplied with an efficient staff of her trained nurses; as was the other board hospital of two hundred beds in Cleveland Street.

Sydney's first distinguished service to the hospital was the provision of a convalescent home. There was none when he began attending meetings, nor was there a single trained nurse in the hospital. The female staff were under the control of a matron, who was the highly respected widow of a solicitor but who had no previous nursing experience. The hospital managers were well aware that a convalescent home was needed, as they understood that a patient often made a much better recovery when given a change of air and scenery.

It was during this time that Lauderdale House in Highgate became vacant. The property is close to Fairseat House, then Sydney's home, near the top of Highgate Hill. Lauderdale House is a significant building which originally belonged to the wife of the

Earl of Lauderdale, a member of the infamous cabal of Charles II. The earl had offered it to the king to enable him to spend time with his mistress Nell Gwynn and their infant son. When Nell wanted the king to give their baby an aristocratic title, she is said to have held the boy out of a first-floor window. "Make him a duke or I drop him," demanded Nell. The king replied, "God save the Earl of Burford!"

Before Sydney took possession of it, Lauderdale House had remained pretty much unchanged since the king had found it convenient for the housing of his various mistresses. So, in order to render it fit for purpose, the building had been skilfully renovated to meet the requirements of its new task; there were large dayrooms and wards for thirty-four beds. Once completed, Sydney handed it over to the governors of Bart's ready to receive its first intake of patients. This was done without any cost to the hospital and remained rent free for seven years.

The Prince of Wales was president of Bart's at that time and opened the convalescent home at Highgate on 8 July 1872, when the princess and many other distinguished people were present. On behalf of the hospital governors, the prince expressed their thanks:

'We all owe you a great debt of gratitude for your immense liberality and are all fully convinced of the advantages the institution is calculated to confer, as an annex to St Bartholomew's, on patients recovering from

159

illness. It has given pleasure to the princess and myself to have a part in these opening ceremonies.'

The convalescent home remained in use until 1880 when all the patients were transferred to the much larger home at Swanley in Kent.

Two years after the Highgate ceremony, at a meeting of the governors presided over by the Prince of Wales, Sydney was unanimously elected treasurer of St Bartholomew's Hospital. It was an unpaid appointment, but what he thought of the post and its duties may be gleaned from his acceptance address. He remarked coyly that he viewed the vote as a testimony to his general public character, 'and a direct expression of confidence in the judgement, temper, and zeal, which I may be able to bring to the discharge of these functions.'

'We inherit this great hospital from the piety of the past. It has done noble service through many generations. It is no small honour to stand in such a line, no light responsibility to keep up for a time that line of faithful help, and to hand on the great inheritance to those who shall come after us, not impoverished or weakened, but richer and stronger for our care.

'For some 750 years this hospital of St Bartholomew has been a centre of help and relief to the poor of this City. Amid social, political, and commercial changes, through dynastic and religious revolutions, it has been a constant witness to that charity which all men alike admire and need. It is a perpetual testimony to a unity which underlies all our diversities, a common feeling and interest which binds us together in spite of the widest differences that can sever us.'

Normally, one would assume that the duties of the treasurer would involve the management of the hospital's funds, the responsibility of personally looking after the estates, houses and landed property of the trust, the supervision of hospital buildings and the care and of receipts and expenditure. However, in those days the treasurer of Bart's Hospital was, in reality, the chief executive of the entire organisation, and this included the management of all officers, staff and other ancillary members of each department.

'This is, in fact, the main portion of the treasurer's charge. The function of the treasurer is to keep in personal relation to them all, and so to form, if I may say so, the common centre which unites and harmonises them, the centre of gravity around which they move.'

Sydney regarded the medical school as, possibly, the most valuable asset of the hospital, and that to keep the unit thriving and efficient would be one of his main endeavours. The hospital represented to him the noblest parts of both science and government; "a work of charity and of mercy which shall not suffer at my hands so far as it is committed to my keeping".

The appointment of the new treasurer was received with great enthusiasm from all quarters, public, medical and surgical and it was summed up neatly by one of the prominent surgeons of the day, Sir James Paget. He wrote to Sydney:

'It will, I believe, be a real happiness to you to find so unbounded a field for humane work, and certainly it will be happy for the hospital that it will be under the guidance of one so devoted to good work, and so experienced in it, as yourself.'

Sir James had entered Bart's Hospital as a student and had passed the better part of his professional career in the hospital and remained there as senior surgeon until his retirement.

Justifiably, a man's worth can really only be judged by his deeds rather than his words, and this was never more true than with Sydney and his achievements as treasurer, from his election in 1874 until his resignation in 1892. During those eighteen years Sydney had to offer himself for re-election on an annual basis but was unanimously re-selected every time.

As a measure of his dedication, Sydney left his home in Highgate with its grounds, open air and other attractions and went to live, periodically, within the precincts of the hospital. He had great plans for Bart's, including many reforms and re-organisation of the hospital system and wanted to give the whole job his best attention. He spent many months closely observing the day-to-day running of the hospital until he knew it inside out. His method of governance was not to issue proclamations and circulars to all and sundry but to communicate with the specifics in a direct fashion. He wrote to the medical staff on matters concerning the office of Administrator of Chloroform, a forerunner of today's Department of Anaesthesiology; he also made provision that patients who were suffering from contagious diseases would be separated from the general patient population and moved to separate wards, something which today would be considered standard practice.

Then came a sweeping proposal: the employment of trained nurses with a fully trained and experienced matron as superintendent. The days of using the highly respected widow of a solicitor were over; something more professional was now required. The sisters of the hospital were all highly regarded but equally highly incompetent. They performed their duties conscientiously, but this was in no way a good substitute for proper knowledge and training.

One of the hospital's main rivals was to the west of them, also on the south side of the river — St Thomas' Hospital. They were already staffed with trained nurses supplied by Miss Florence Nightingale. So, persuading the Bart's hospital governors to grant a retiring pension to the current matron, Sydney approached Miss Nightingale to help find a worthy successor. She eventually located a suitable replacement who hailed all the way from Montreal, Canada, and she also proposed four trained nurses for her staff. Miss Nightingale also had cause to write to Sydney in support of his project:

'I should ere this, had I not been afraid of troubling your well-filled time, have seized the opportunity of giving you joy, and the nursing cause too, for your wise and efficient measures for improving the nursing.

'...I think I am as anxious for your success as for our own. Or rather it is all one, the good nursing cause, so furthered by you. But you would not think much of our training if we had always a stock of people 'trained at a moment's notice,' as the advertisements have it, on hand to offer. God speed St Bartholomew's nursing and its treasurer! Ever your faithful servant, Florence Nightingale.'

Sadly, the lady from Montreal soon departed. The untrained sisters and nurses, still in attendance, were proving difficult to manage, nor would they work harmoniously with the newly arrived, trained nurses. So, Sydney had to start again from scratch to fill the vacant post. After a seemingly fruitless search he was introduced to a Mrs Gladstone who had set up her own convalescent home in Woodford, Essex, and was frequently to be found working at the London Hospital in Whitechapel. In that hospital, in charge of a ward with forty beds, was a certain Miss Ethel Manson, who Mrs Gladstone strongly recommended to Sydney would make a suitable matron for Bart's. On that recommendation, Sydney then visited the London Hospital twice, visiting Miss Manson's ward on the pretext of being someone who was interested in nursing. He liked what he saw in Miss Manson, considering her very suitable for the role; the main issue was going to be persuading the two hundred hospital governors to agree with his choice. Ever the diplomat, instead of forcing them to make a decision straightaway, Sydney convinced them to allow the new matron a three-month trial, after which they could either ratify or reject his choice. Such was the impression made by Miss Manson that she was unanimously confirmed at the end of her probation.

Despite the total agreement of the hospital's governors of the appointment, there were objections raised by several of the senior doctors as to Ethel's selection as matron. These were mainly on the grounds that she was too young and pretty; Sydney's response to this:

'The first fault time will remedy; the second I do not regard as altogether a fault, for I think a kind, genial, sympathising word from a pretty woman is very acceptable to a sick patient.'

Ethel Manson continued as matron of Bart's for several years, working to everyone's complete satisfaction and devoting herself fully to the job in hand. She also developed the Nurses' Training School only eventually leaving to get married.

One of the more unlikely tasks of the hospital treasurer involved dealing with certain legal matters pertaining to the hospital's estates. A long time prior to Sydney's attachment to the institution, the Crown had granted the hospital the tithe of the parish of Christchurch in Dorset. The essence of which meant that there was a legal claim to half a crown of every pound from property rental from within the town which would go to the hospital. For some reason this had been allowed to lapse over time to the point where the hospital was now only receiving tuppence instead of half a crown. A newly convened board of governors decided that the time had come to revive the old claim as of right. The tithe-payers took exception to this and refused to pay. So, the hospital's governors put a case before the Chancery but, as so often happens even now, this application got caught up in the system. Sydney, always looking for a compromise, and, in an effort to move things along, made the offer of terms of ten pence in every pound. Finally, this offer was accepted by the people of Christchurch and the hospital began to profit to the extent of an additional £1,800 per year.

In the past, Bart's Hospital had not possessed a dedicated lecture room or a well-ventilated dissecting room for medical student training. This problem was brought before the governors who soon agreed to plans which Sydney had prepared. There was to be a new dissecting room five times larger than before, a library, classrooms and a museum. These were all built on the site of the old building facing West Smithfield at a cost of £70,000. It was considered such a landmark achievement that an opening ceremony was held on 3 November 1879 presided over by the Prince of Wales and attended by other distinguished guests. Sydney, as the mouthpiece of the governors, delivered an address both historical and explanatory:

'The governors, after a full and most careful consideration of the whole question, gave permission for the construction of a new library, practical classrooms, a new museum, a new anatomical theatre to accommodate four hundred students, a new chemical and medical theatre for two hundred, with new dissecting rooms constructed on the most approved modern sanitary principles, enabling more than two hundred pupils to pursue their studies at the same time.'

He went on to detail other important particulars of the new reforming energies at work in the hospital. The convalescent home would shortly be transferred out to Kent with a doubling of the number of beds. The training of skilled nurses had begun in 1877, and thirty probationers were currently working in the wards and attending lectures from professors of medicine and surgery.

'I trust that Your Royal Highness as President will sympathise with me as Treasurer, and with the governors and staff of the hospital, in the feeling that we are therefore bound in our own way to do all that we can to carry forward in the best possible manner the good work handed down to us, in order that our royal charity may continue to relieve and to cure a constantly increasing number of the sick poor of this great metropolis.'

To signify his approval, the Prince of Wales then declared the new buildings open and it must be noted that the royal presence in this instance was not solely ornamental but also proved to be very profitable for the hospital. As a result, the number of students at the medical school greatly increased and it was not long before the total exceeded that of rival Guy's Hospital and every other medical school in England. Before 1873 the annual register of students had varied from fifty to seventy. By 1878 it had risen to one hundred and fifty-three.

Having also secured his trained nurses, Sydney thought it only right and proper to look after their health and welfare. The only home they had was the hospital wards and their bedrooms which were nothing more than windowless dens built out of the staircase. The night duty nurses would get into beds only recently vacated by the day nurses and some even slept on the wards. The whole situation was very crude, primitive and unnecessarily insanitary. There had been a previous, unsuccessful attempt to improve things when several houses, some very old, and even a pub, had been turned into dormitories. The matron's report concerning this accommodation had been filled with the most shocking and horrific detail with the result that other houses were quickly located for the purpose. These replacement houses were some two hundred years old but were eventually made sanitary and habitable.

In the spring of 1892, Sydney, now in his seventieth year, began to feel that his work at the hospital was starting to take its toll on him and he was now advised by his physician to resign from his office of treasurer and start taking life a little more easily. Surprisingly, and probably because he was beginning to feel the strain, on 20 June 1892 Sydney sent his letter of resignation to the president and governors of the hospital.

'The rules of the medical hospital provide that no medical officer shall hold office after sixty-five. I have long since passed that age. After fifty-five years of work in the City of London, I have to thank God that I still enjoy good health, but my friends and medical adviser strongly recommend me to pass the winter on the Riviera.

'Under the circumstances I feel it to be my duty to intimate to you that I do not propose to offer myself for re-election on Thursday, July 28th next, being election day. My work here for the last eighteen years has been as great pleasure to me, and a constant labour of love. I am encouraged in my retirement by the belief that I leave the hospital to the guidance of my successor in a much stronger position, both as a place of relief and cure of sick patients, and also as an educational institution, than when I found it in 1874.'

The reply came from the Prince of Wales by the hand of Sir Francis Knollys:

'His Royal Highness the President directs me to assure you of the very sincere regret which he experiences at learning that circumstances have compelled you to come to this decision, and to express to you his sense of the great loss which the hospital will sustain by your withdrawal from an office which you have most ably filled, with so much advantage to the institution and with the entire confidence of the Prince and the Court of Governors, for the last eighteen years.

'You will have the satisfaction of retiring with the knowledge that during that long period the prosperity of the institution has largely increased and (as you observe) that the hospital has made rapid progress in its endeavour to be, not only a place of cure and relief, but one likewise for the advancement of education and instruction.'

The regret of the medical profession as a whole was expressed at length by *The Lancet*; reciting Sydney's long list of achievements and improvements, and remarking that 'it is to his credit that he perceived their necessity, and so husbanded the resources that they could be easily executed'. *The Times* newspaper echoed the sentiments of the general public, giving a slightly incomplete account of his work and rightly considering that his good deeds were his best eulogy. The governors of Bart's Hospital resolved unanimously:

'That this Court receives his resignation with unfeigned regret: that, reviewing the period of his treasurer-ship, the Court has the utmost pleasure in acknowledging that the great advance in the material prosperity of the institution, and in its arrangements for ministering to the relief of the objects of its charity, is in no small measure due to Sir Sydney Waterlow's great business capacity, his singular administrative ability, and to his zealous devotion to the interests of the hospital and the well-being of the sick and suffering poor.

'That the Court begs leave to offer to Sir Sydney Waterlow its most cordial and grateful thanks for his invaluable services in the past eighteen years, and desires to express its earnest hope that during a prolonged life he may be blessed with continued health and happiness.

'(Signed) ALBERT EDWARD, *President.*'

As a memorial to his treasurer-ship he was asked by the hospital's governors, medical, surgical and nursing staff to sit for his portrait, to be hung in the great hall of the hospital. Among the subscribers were the Prince of Wales, 166 governors including Lord Derby, the Lord Mayor, surgeon Sir James Paget and the entire hospital staff. The portrait was painted by Professor Sir Hubert von Herkomer and the picture now hangs in the Guildhall Art Gallery.

At the risk of sounding too maudlin, the following is a list of the improvements made at the hospital during Sydney's term as treasurer:

• Annual income of the hospital increased from £53,104 to £79,703

• Formation of special departments for ophthalmic, orthopaedic, skin, ear and throat diseases

• Establishment of an electrical department, with complete apparatus and a medical officer in charge

- Medical and surgical staff numbers increased from thirty to fifty-seven

- School buildings rebuilt at a cost of £50,000 and the number of students increasing from 223 to 469

- Construction of isolation rooms for infectious and contagious diseases

- Complete re-organisation of the nursing department, including the establishment of a training school for nurses; improved arrangements for the domestic comforts of the nurses, with bedrooms in a home away from the wards

- Female nursing staff increased from 116 to 232 including training for the nurses

- The establishment of an institution for supplying the public with fully trained and competent nurses

- Provision of a convalescent home at Highgate, a gift from Sydney, with thirty-two beds, subsequently superseded by a much larger home at Swanley with seventy beds

- Installation of hydraulic lifts in the four wings of the hospital

- Improved sanitation

There was no doubt that Sydney took great pleasure and pride in his deeds while at the hospital. However, he would very rarely, if ever, speak about his work to acquaintances or anyone else who did not show any concern for such things. To friends, he would refer to the achievements of those eighteen years with gratitude that he had been able to accomplish so much. Although generally when asked about it he would say, "No, you are only interested in the treasurer-ship of Bartholomew's because I was the treasurer. You don't really want to know about it for its own sake".

There is, however, one item lacking from the list of improvements during Sydney's time in office. It is something which is never easy to measure, but one which is certainly noticeable by its absence — public confidence. This confidence grew as the work progressed and reached a height which had never been experienced before. The reforms started by Sydney were the building blocks of the hospital that St Bartholomew's is today.

CHAPTER XII
HOSPITAL SUNDAY FUND

Closely related to Sydney's work with Bart's Hospital was his work in connection with the Metropolitan Hospital Fund. From 1863 when, as alderman, he became ex-officio governor of Bart's Hospital right through to the end of his active life, he was always involved in one way or another working for the betterment of hospitals. In Victorian London there were more than two hundred hospitals of one type or another, but only three or four of these were able to sustain their existence from their endowments or anything but voluntary contributions. It was this contribution system that Sydney endeavoured to see maintained, but he also understood that it would need a great deal of work to make this happen.

The Sunday Hospital Fund scheme was first conceived by Richard B. Martin and Sir Edmund Currie. Near the end of 1872, during Sydney's tenure as lord mayor, these two gentlemen had approached him with a suggestion for making an annual collection in the metropolitan churches on a fixed day each year. The funds would then be divided to supplement the funds of the hospitals and dispensaries of London. Sydney was very taken with the idea and decided to act upon it, welcoming it as something more than aiding hospital funds by commercial venture. In his view this was an opportunity for churches and congregations of all kinds, regardless of theological persuasion, to unite in an act of Christian benevolence for one Sunday every year.

The scheme had no lack of supporters. Among those offering their services were the Rev. Canon Miller of Greenwich and Dr Wakely, editor of *The Lancet*. Even more prominent medical professionals like Sir William Gull, physician to Queen Victoria, and Sir James Paget, eminent surgeon and pathologist, befriended the scheme, as did Archbishop Manning and the Bishops of Winchester and Rochester. From the secular division of the community the Earl of Derby and Baroness Angela Burdett-Coutts also both had a share of the scheme.

The Hospital Sunday Fund was formally initiated at a meeting held in the Egyptian Hall of the Mansion House in January 1873, when Sydney, as lord mayor, was appointed president and treasurer. The first collection, taken the following June, raised £28,000 (approximately equivalent to £3 million in 2020), but the moment the money was in the treasurer's hands the distribution problems began. The main issues being which hospitals were to benefit, and in what proportion? These problems were to continue throughout Sydney's tenure in office and appeared to be, often as now,

175

inseparable from the general administration of this type of charity.

As with so many of the complications he encountered, Sydney took a business-type view of the situation; it was not in his nature to do otherwise. It was decided that the fairest method was to request those hospitals wishing to benefit from the fund to send in an application accompanied by a statement of accounts which were to be drawn up to a standardised format. A hospital which was extravagantly managed found its stipends reduced or totally withheld. Sydney had very definite ideas as to the ratio which ought to exist between income and expenses and what proportion was to be considered reasonable, and the rule required that the accounts submitted were to cover the three years prior to the application. This was readily agreed to by representatives of all the leading hospitals and confirmed by the council of the trust. The accounts were examined in minute detail and this, together with other measures applied during the process, produced better economy and more efficient management in the various hospitals. The refusal of the committee to donate a grant to any particular hospital left a smear on that hospital's reputation which in turn affected any other donations the hospital could expect to receive. This then had the result that the hospital in question was forced to mend its ways in order to reap the benefits of the system.

At the end of his lord mayoralty, Sydney ceased to be president of the trust, and from then on each lord mayor became the ex-officio president. However, Sydney was then elected vice-president and chairman of the distribution committee and remained in office for twenty-four years. He and his colleagues certainly practised what they preached in terms of economy. They managed the fund at a cost of 2.5 per cent of the amount received; nevertheless, there was at least one hospital where the management expenses amounted to twenty-five per cent of the money spent for the support of patients.

Sydney wrote in his journal:

'Nothing that I have undertaken has been more satisfactory to me than the gradual process which the Hospital Sunday Fund has made in the public mind. In 1873 we had 1,072 congregations at which services were held and collections made on the day fixed by the council, whereas by 1894 the number of contributing congregations had risen gradually to 1,799. While the total receipts for congregational collections, legacies, and special donations, only reached in 1873 the sum of £27,700, in 1874 the sum of £43,679 was received from the same sources, and in 1895 the large sum of £60,361 (£7.8 million).

'Although the money received gradually increased, the number of institutions applying for assistance increased in even a larger ratio. In 1873 the money was divided amongst 77 hospitals, dispensaries, etc., while 182 institutions received grants in 1894.'

Occasionally public meetings were held to allow the general public to witness the claims processes at first hand. Sydney recalls that these were started:

'...from a feeling that the public generally did not grasp the duties and responsibilities which fell upon them in supporting the hospitals and dispensaries of the country in which they lived. In America the maintenance of the hospitals and dispensaries is cast as a tax upon the population. It is not so in this country, and I hope it may never be so, but that the voluntary principle will always be maintained. As I have said, I do not think the public thoroughly comprehend the duty devolving upon them. I want now to make everyone feel that that which they have to lean upon in the time of their trouble they should not forget in the time of health.'

Other funds of a similar nature and intent started appearing, namely the Hospital Saturday Fund and the Prince of Wales' Fund. These were not intended to be rivals for the original as they also had the ultimate purpose of providing funds to the hospitals, but there was a certain amount of latent competitiveness between them all. The Saturday Fund began about a year after the Sunday Fund, collecting their revenue mainly from weekly workshop visits and street collections, and in 1896 this amounted to £21,614 (£2.9 million equivalent in 2020).

The fund reached its twenty-fifth anniversary in 1898, and on 3 August that year a meeting was held at the Mansion House presided over by Sydney. The receipts for that year had been £38,741, a decrease compared to previous years, but one which did not seem to trouble Sydney. In addition to the supplied funds, some twelve hospitals had also leaned a little on the committee for something other than money. Members of these institutions had made representations at the Mansion House meeting. Sydney observed that:

'scarcely any of the gentlemen who came to them left the committee without expressing their appreciation of the advantages they derived from a conference with the committee, who had for so many years been engaged in discussing whether this or that institution was conducted in a manner which was not only efficient, but reasonably economical.'

Economy and efficiency were the two principal conditions adhered to, and, in general, standards were high in both regards. These standards were set by Sydney himself and the audits of the hospitals' accounts were rigid in the extreme. However, as a result, the hospitals and their administrations profited, but above all the patients profited because of the high proportion of the money being spent on their care.

The resulting effects of the regime were far-reaching. The sums of money distributed amongst the nearly two hundred hospitals became only one benefit bestowed on them. The total income of each hospital usually increased by considerably more than the sum total of the money allocated to it. By 1907 the annual receipts had grown to £78,651 (£9.6 million), of which £42,618 came from churches and their congregations, and £35,833 from gifts, legacies and investments. The number of hospitals, dispensaries and nursing institutions to benefit from this sum had also increased to two hundred and forty-three.

Since his first involvement with Bart's Hospital, Sydney had the welfare of hospitals in his blood. Despite his apparent hard exterior, he had a rare tenderness towards all who suffered through illness; the relief of which was almost a sacred duty to him to the extent that he never went anywhere without enquiring into the local hospital's state of affairs. Even in places as far afield as Cairo he worked with the Khedive to secure trained nurses for the local hospitals in the vicinity. In New York, his first visits were to the local hospitals; in Cannes, where he had bought a villa for his winter residence, he set up an English hospital nearby to which he not only gave money but his close and personal attention for many years. The nurses for this particular hospital were brought out from London, and the permanent medical staff, were the best, as could be found locally. The building itself was not substantial by any means but was certainly of the highest standard possible. His involvement in Cannes made him very much admired, respected and even loved by all those involved. He would listen patiently to the head nurse, as she was the expert, when her opinion differed from Sydney's on any point, and he would willingly give way to her when convinced of her argument. But he had to be convinced, and to the amateur he would not listen at all. Why should he? He had more important things to do with his time.

CHAPTER XIII
AMERICA & AROUND THE WORLD

'I have been a great traveller,' Sydney was heard to remark on more than one occasion, and this certainly cannot be disputed. By the turn of the century, he had circumnavigated the globe, crossed the Atlantic half a dozen times, crossed the North American continent three times and had toured Egypt and India. Even by today's standards that would be considered quite a list, but even more remarkable given the relative complexity of travel logistics over a century ago.

Sydney's first journey to the USA was in 1876 as commissioner to the World's 'Centennial' Exhibition in Philadelphia when he was accompanied by his eldest son, Philip. His triumphal return home was overshadowed by the news of the death of his father, James, of whose illness he had heard nothing until he received a telegram on arriving in Queenstown, Ireland. James Waterlow had died peacefully at home on 11 July 1876, but the loss of his father hit Sydney badly, "for no man was ever more beloved or esteemed by all who knew him"; he had been, after all, the original 'Waterlow' of the family firm and a source of great inspiration and endeavour.

After the death of his wife, Anna Maria, on 21 January 1880, the following year found Sydney undertaking a journey which was to be his most eventful. He left Moville, County Donegal in August on the Allan Line steamship *Circassian*, taking with him his two daughters, Ruth and Hilda and his son, Paul. They made "a very rapid passage across the Atlantic" landing in Quebec eight days later. On arrival at the quayside, to his surprise, Sydney was greeted by one of the tenants whom the Duke of Buccleuch had evicted from his farm for the offence of voting for Sydney when he had stood against the duke in the parliamentary election of 1868. Having been driven from his farm for the exercising of his electoral rights, the ex-tenant had now found a lucrative new life for himself in Canada.

Also, during his time in Canada, Sydney had occasion to be interviewed by various reporters. One of these encounters took place in Toronto and the resulting article concluded by describing him as a 'level-headed man'. Sydney took this to be an expression of the reporter's discontent, "but they assured me that, in American parlance, it was as great a compliment as he could have paid me"; clearly the use of the term 'American' was intended to encompass the Canadian as well as the American nation.

On this particular excursion it was originally intended that Chicago was to be the limit of Sydney's journey. However, a friend who was traffic superintendent on the Rock Island Line from Chicago to Omaha, Nebraska assured him that he would not get a complete, total appreciation of America unless he visited San Francisco. A rail journey of some four or five days "seemed a terrible undertaking for such a party as mine", but his friend promised to make the adventure as comfortable as possible within his capabilities, and so Sydney was swayed.

The Rock Island trains were equipped with sleeping berths and restaurant cars as were the trains on the Union Pacific Railroad. However, on the Central Pacific, the party had to be content with comfortable accommodation and "catching their meals at the roadside restaurants". In Salt Lake City they found the streets lit by electricity, unknown in England, except experimentally, until many years later. Sydney even visited a baby show commenting that he thought the babies much finer specimens of humanity than their mothers!

The rest of the journey was appreciated, particularly in terms of the scenery on display, but Sydney still found himself anxious to be going home. However, what happened next is best described in his own words:

'Although my stay in San Francisco did not exceed ten days, I was fortunate in obtaining an introduction to a lady who, a few months afterwards, came over to England and became my wife. We were married in Paris in March 1882, and from that time I have always felt that the friend who persuaded me to go to San Francisco was my greatest benefactor.' This was an opinion shared by many of Sydney's friends.

This lady was Miss Margaret Hamilton, second daughter of the late William Hamilton of Napa, California. It turned out to be a union of lifelong happiness for both parties.

Naturally enough, the next transatlantic journey was back to California. Sir Sydney and (the now) Lady Waterlow had a desire to travel around the world, and San Francisco presented itself as a convenient stopping place. They left London in the autumn of 1883 as Sydney had, by then, "practically retired from business", and Margaret's return to San Francisco turned out to be an event of some interest. Anglo-American marriages were quite a rarity back then and this one was an especially unusual example. Miss Margaret Hamilton had married an Englishman of distinction twice her own age; eighteen months had passed and she was still a bride!

The couple stayed in San Francisco for two weeks when they were joined by a young lady friend of Margaret's and the three of them then sailed across the Pacific for nineteen days to Yokohama. They spent two weeks in Japan and then on to Hong Kong and Canton in China. At that time there was considerable tension in the area and their ship was escorted on the final leg of their journey by European and American warships.

'The tables in the bedrooms were covered with firearms. The house of a merchant with whom we stayed was guarded by patrols all through the night'. Yet, 'we could not resist visiting the trading parts of the City of Canton, and the City of Boats in the river, although we were warned we should go at our peril'. Fortunately, they came to no harm other than having to endure some jeering and the odd insult.

From Canton to Saigon, then on to Singapore and Colombo where they were deluged with tropical storms. To escape the worst of the weather, they travelled to Madras, having lunch with the Governor, Sir Mountstuart Grant-Duff; they also came within a measurable distance of being drowned in the surf when they re-embarked on their French steamer. When they eventually reached the deck of the ship "friends who had been watching us dropped down on their knees, thanking God for our safety".

They arrived in Calcutta on Christmas Eve 1883, staying there over the festive period as guests of Henry Gladstone, the third son of the then British Prime Minister, William E. Gladstone. From Calcutta they continued on to Benares, Cawnpore (Kanpur), Lucknow, Delhi and Agra, where "morning, noon, and night" they visited the Taj Mahal; on one occasion the sun and moon obligingly lighting up different sides of the majestic edifice at the same time.

'The ladies were so fascinated that they remained in the temple until past eleven at night, chanting hymns which echoed and re-echoed in the dome.'

Eventually sailing out of Bombay, they ran into an outbreak of cholera at Port Saïd and were obliged to endure quarantine at Marseilles. This involved a compulsory eight days out at sea and twenty-four hours sitting outside the port. To make the eight days at sea easier to bear, the captain went at half speed through the Mediterranean and the passengers appeared to appreciate it. On arrival in Marseilles, Sydney found telegrams requiring his immediate presence in the House of Commons for an important division of the House. The British authorities at the port argued for Sydney to be allowed to disembark immediately, but the French authorities were having none of it. Luckily, the division of the House was delayed and Sydney arrived back in London in time to cast his vote.

In 1886, Sydney and Margaret returned to America accompanied by Sydney's daughters, Hilda and Celia. They visited Charles Crocker, one of the founders of the Central Pacific Railroad and it was here that Hilda met Alfred Ford of San Francisco and they were married shortly afterwards, eventually producing six sons!

Finally, the trip took them east across the country on a three-thousand-mile journey to Boston, Massachusetts where they stayed with Robert Treat, a

Boston philanthropist. He took them on a tour of the city including showing them two streets, one named 'Sydney', the other 'Waterlow'. On both these streets had been built large blocks of tenement houses which had been constructed using the plans originally designed for the working men's dwellings in London.

CHAPTER XIV
CITY & GUILDS INSTITUTE

As early as 1869 Sydney began to turn his thoughts to the matter of technical education and started to enquire of his many informed contacts as to the current state of affairs in schools. At that time, there was no such thing as technical education in Britain, certainly nowhere near the level that exists now.

However modest and low-key these initial enquiries might have been, the whole idea was considered somewhat visionary and Sydney became almost revered for even making the initial suggestion. For up to sixteen years previously the only scientific classes available in Britain were those in connection with the Committee of the East Lincolnshire Union of Institutions or through evening classes. It was in 1853 that the work of the Science and Art Departments of the Committee of the Council on Education began.

The lack of technical training in Britain was made even more evident at the Paris Exhibition of 1867, where Sydney himself was a juror for Great Britain. The British people were to realise, to their dismay, there was a serious deficiency of technical training and scientific knowledge within the country. From that moment on there was a concerted effort to increase and improve evening classes for scientific instruction.

No doubt inspired by what he had seen in Paris, Sydney decided to take up the challenge. It was slow work, naturally, as he had to find the time for it amongst all his other projects and business ventures. Through Sydney's Liberal Party connections, one person stepped forward to offer assistance; Auberon Herbert, brother of the 4th Earl of Carnarvon, arranged for a meeting of working men's clubs as it would be from there that the strongest opposition of the plan was likely to come. However, it was not until 1872 that Sydney managed to assemble a small committee in the City to discuss the matter. One alderman objected; he did not want any of his men to be taught chemistry and other matters by which they would be able to discover all the secrets of his business; it would be 'monstrous'. Sadly, history does not recall his name, but it is believed that he was a dealer in paints, colours and varnishes.

Once again, the much-criticised livery companies were at the forefront of the reform movement. It was they, especially the Clothworkers, who did much to call attention to the subject, particularly public attention. The members discussed the subject among themselves and appointed a committee to consider the wisdom of encouraging the cloth trade to teach the techniques of their craft, as well as involving other skills and trades to consider the same. Eventually, a meeting was held in the Mansion House with Sydney in the Chair; at that meeting he proposed the construction of a building where technical schools for the children of the working classes could be held. However, it was Welsh educationalist, Owen Roberts, who put himself at the head of the livery companies in their struggles for technical education. The Drapers decided to join forces with the Clothworkers in the venture, and in December 1876 Sydney submitted the following motion to the Court of the Clothworkers' Company:

'That while the Court has every reason to be gratified with the success which is attending its experiments in providing improved industrial training for the clothworkers of Yorkshire and the West of England, in connection with the Yorkshire and Bristol Colleges of Science, it is desirable that the Clothworkers' Company should initiate a movement for establishing in London a City Guilds' Industrial Institute or University, with affiliated branches for the local centres of the various industries in the suburbs and the provinces generally, where the latest appliances of the science to the development of the trades and manufactures generally may receive practical illustration and impetus, as the most effective substitute for the superseded system of apprenticeship, such an important element of, and so strongly inculcated by, the by-laws of all the guilds of London, which was, in fact, the technical education of former days; and that this Court is prepared to devote the sum of £2,000 per annum towards establishing such an institution on a scale proportionate to the necessities of the time and to the wealth and intelligence of the associated companies of London, in extension of the Gresham College or otherwise, as may be determined hereafter; and provided that satisfactory subscriptions are promised by other livery companies.'

So, in one, rather long, sentence Sydney had grouped together his plans, aspirations and, perhaps, one regret; in the reference to "the superseded system of apprenticeship" he recalled his affection for his early days and for a system that was now obsolete. Nevertheless, the motion was carried without dissent and the grant of £2,000 a year was the first money ever voted by any public body for providing technical education facilities in London. Even after Sydney's death, the furtherance of technical education continued at a pace, but that he was one of the earliest promoters of technical education is something which cannot be forgotten.

So, the City and Guilds of London Institute grew out of the Clothworkers' initial gift of £2,000 per year. They and the Drapers' Company held a conference shortly after the initial meeting, again with Sydney presiding, and it was resolved:

'That this joint committee of Drapers and Clothworkers is of opinion that the City Companies generally should unite in promoting a national system of technical education by forming a City Guilds Technical Institute or University, with affiliated branches for the local centres of various trades and industries in the suburbs and provinces generally.'

They put before themselves five leading objects:

'1. To provide technical instruction in those manufacturing arts and industries in London in which such instruction is not now provided.

2. To assist in the development of places of technical instruction already in London.

3. To assist in establishing and maintaining schools of technical instruction in the provincial centres of trade.

4. The companies do not propose to ask for government assistance.

5. To secure a prominent site in London for the erection of a college for the education of teachers.'

In the loosest of terms, this could almost be considered the original charter of the City and Guilds programme.

Sydney's next target was the Mercers' Company of which Roundell Palmer, Lord Selborne, was the most influential member. After some gentle persuasion, the Mercers donated £3,000 a year and Selborne became Chairman of the Council of the Guilds Technical Institute.

At the end of 1876 the Clothworkers issued their draft scheme. Their central idea was combined action by the livery companies and by the Corporation of London. Disposing of great riches, the companies and the corporation, assuming that they all co-operated freely, might well dispense with government aid in any form. A building fund of £60,000 and an annual income of £20,000 were then thought to be perfectly adequate. But public opinion was still apathetic, and some of the companies remained somewhat detached and continued to be so for quite a while.

Despite this, Sydney continued his crusade, and his efforts were by and large successful. Some companies needed little or no persuasion, and while some others were a little more reticent, they would come around eventually. But by June 1877, the pledges of assistance had become so numerous that Lord Selborne wrote to Sydney suggesting that the representative committee of the proposed college needed a practical person to draw up a practicable scheme. He put forward a man by the name of Major Donnelly, a veteran of the Crimean War who had been unsuccessfully nominated, quite controversially, for the Victoria Cross. Sydney was quick to agree with the choice and Donnelly immediately prepared a report which was not only elaborate but was also creative, detailed and business-like. Other reports were also prepared by Lord Playfair (scientist and Liberal politician), Captain Douglas Galton (engineer), Sir Isaac Lowthian Bell (metallurgist and industrial chemist), Professor Thomas Huxley (biologist and anthropologist) and Sir William Armstrong (engineer and industrialist), later Baron Armstrong of Cragside.

In July 1877, armed with these reports, the representative committees drafted a constitution for the proposed institute and presented it to the subscribing companies. At that time the Clothworkers, Mercers, Drapers, Fishmongers and Goldsmiths were each contributing £2,000 a year to the scheme; there were also smaller pledges from other companies bringing the total annual income up to £11,582 (£1.3 million). An executive committee was appointed which reported in at the end of the year, setting forth plans for the organisation of the technical college and pressing the livery companies to immediately vote for a sum of not less than £25,000 a year to establish the enterprise on a sure footing. Although the Clothworkers, Drapers, Mercers, Fishmongers and Goldsmiths did eventually all double their subscriptions, the less enthusiastic companies stayed defiant and the progress of the scheme remained pedestrian. It was not until 17 March 1879 that the board of governors of the institute elected Sydney as treasurer; a post he held until June 1891.

The Corporation of London still had no share in any of this; there were still too many members who considered the proposal too 'visionary'. In March 1880, Lord Selborne, Sir Frederick Bramwell and Sydney, as treasurer, wrote to the lord mayor asking for a definite statement of intentions toward the scheme from the Corporation. A site had already been chosen for the building to occupy which had been agreed with the commissioners of the Great Exhibition of 1851, but a lease for it had to be granted, but to whom? So far the name of the City had been incorporated in the title of the organisation in the hope that the City would finally come in, but the institute now had to be legally registered and a decision had to be taken one way or the other.

In April, the letter was referred to the Finance Committee of the Corporation, who sat on it for seven months; they finally sent a reply in November to the effect that the institute ought to be supported financially by the livery companies and not by the City. The full court met on 2 December when there was a somewhat heated debate. The fact that the government had given the institute a site worth £100,000 on lease for 990 years at a peppercorn rent was pressed upon the court in the hope that it would shame them into relenting. Sydney also used his influence as alderman, appealing to the pride of the citizens and Corporation of London, to argue that if the City companies were able to subscribe even twice the £2,000 which they were being asked for it would be a mere drop in the ocean to them. He explained that in Europe, where many of the top technical schools existed, the municipal authorities gave a third of the total cost and the government another third. These enabled the fees to be kept affordable for those whom the education and training was meant to benefit most. He also added that the current contributing companies wanted the corporation to also contribute, not just for the sake of the money, but so that the other companies and the corporation could be associated with such a noble cause.

Sydney's diplomatic plea had the desired effect, an amendment was carried and the institute was built and opened in 1884 with an income of £35,000 per year. The Finsbury College had also been opened in 1883 at a total cost of £40,000, inclusive of all necessary equipment. By the turn of the century there was also the South London School of Technical Art, the Leather Trades School in Bethnal Green Road and the annual technological examinations in sixty different subjects. All this had happened within ten years of the initial draft scheme having been proposed. At the time, the progress was perceived as being far too slow, especially to Sydney, but given what had been achieved this was something which was nothing short of extraordinary.

While Sydney may not necessarily be regarded as a pioneer in technical education, he was certainly one of those who championed its cause on a large scale. The first Royal Commission appointed into the subject began its investigation in 1880. The Guilds Institute was, naturally, already in existence and as treasurer of the institute, he was examined by them. He was asked to give an account of the whole process and his first effort was to impress on them the fact that he and his associates had studied the European systems thoroughly before attempting to construct their own. They had not merely adapted an existing model but rather had drawn the best parts from each and adapted the whole as needs saw fit. Among the results of this commission was the founding of further technical colleges in Glasgow, Bristol, Bradford, Manchester, Huddersfield, Sheffield and Halifax.

In 1884, however, the City and Guilds Institute of London underwent a minor crisis. The Drapers' Company had become dissatisfied with the arrangement and withdrew its £4,000 annual subscription and this was followed shortly after by some of the smaller companies. The executive committee made an urgent appeal for more funds; the institute was already expanding rapidly but its funds were now shrinking, and the committee set out a minimum income of £40,000 by which the organisation would need to keep running. Certain companies rallied round, including the Clothworkers' who raised their annual subscription to £4,000. On the strength of this minor crisis, Professor Thomas Huxley thought it pertinent to utter a grave warning:

'This country has dropped astern in the race for want of the education which is obtained elsewhere in the highest branches of industry and commerce. It has dropped astern in the race for want of instruction in technical education given elsewhere to the artisan, and if we desire to have every chance to keep up that industrial predominance which was the foundation of the empire, and which, if it fails, will cause the whole fabric of the state to crumble; if we desire to see want and pauperism less common than, unfortunately, they are at present, we must remember that it is only possible by the organisation of industry in the manner in which we understand organisation in science, by straining every nerve to train the intelligence that has served industry, to its highest point, and to keep the industrial products of England at the head of the markets of the world.'

Fortunately, common sense prevailed and the finances of the institute began to improve. Two years after the appeal from the executive committee, the income had risen to £29,350, of which the Goldsmiths gave £6,000, Drapers - £4,500, Clothworkers and Fishmongers £4,000 each and the Mercers £3,000. Ten years later the income to the institute from the livery companies amounted to £453,435. Three years prior to that, Sydney resigned his post as treasurer but, on the recommendation of the Prince of Wales, the council chose Sydney as vice president.

'After my retirement from the position of treasurer, I was unable to give much time or attention to the work of the institute, or to the various movements which were then being organised for the purpose of promoting technical education throughout the country. Although I regretted my inability, this regret was considerably mitigated by the feeling that so many other men, of greater scientific knowledge and more eminent public position than myself, had put their hands to the plough, and, having recognised the importance of the work, were willing to give both time and ability to promoting it.

'I was especially gratified to think that the London County Council had given this subject their attention, and clearly indicated a desire to utilise the funds at their disposal in the establishment of a Technical Education Board, as well as furthering the object in many other ways. It was also cheering to know that a portion of the funds arising from the City Parochial Charities would be applicable for the same purposes.

'It may be that some years must elapse before technical education in this country can hope to compare favourably with that which has been for so many years in operation on the continent, and especially in Germany. But one need not, I think, despair. The work is being forwarded in many directions, and I hope I may live to feel that the time and attention I gave to the subject from 1869 to 1890 have not been entirely thrown away.'

CHAPTER XV
THE WESTMINSTER SCHOOLS

Sydney's journey into education was not entirely confined to the more mature technical aspects. His involvement with the Westminster schools, much like the battle for the City and Guilds Institute, was one which, yet again, involved the Corporation of the City of London; the Corporation of which Sydney was still a member and had already given many years of his life.

Within the City of Westminster and the nearby parish of Chelsea there existed four old educational endowments. The oldest of these, known as Emanuel Hospital, had been founded in 1594 by a Lady Dacre who had large estates in Yorkshire and land and properties in Westminster and elsewhere. After that came St Margaret's Hospital, founded in 1633 under charter from Charles I, and it was in the buildings of this hospital that the schools were first opened. The third was Palmer's Hospital, endowed by a Rev. J. Palmer in 1654. Finally, there was Hill's Grammar School which began life in 1674 under a charter from one Emery Hill, a brewer and benefactor from Westminster.

Of these four, by far the most important and wealthy was the Emanuel Hospital. Its revenues were entirely under the control of the aldermen of the Corporation of London who, each in turn, nominated a child to be clothed, educated and boarded free of charge, paid for by the Corporation. Sadly, the other three establishments had been so badly neglected that in all the four schools there was no more than sixty children, boys and girls, and with the total income from the endowments amounting to only £5,000 per year. As a result of this, a scheme was put before Parliament in 1873 for the re-organisation and re-development of the schools; consolidating all four and putting them under the control of one board of governors and under the authority of the Endowed Schools Commissioners. Naturally, this scheme received strong opposition from the City aldermen who were unwilling to part with any of their authority or prerogatives. They objected to the provision for two-thirds paying scholars and they did everything they could to oppose the bill going through Parliament, even using the City solicitor to act on behalf of the corporation. Even though this was a relatively local matter for London, and at a time when attendance and voting in the House was a good deal less rigorous than it is today, all members of the House, including those who had no connection with London, were supplied with documents and arguments against the proposed scheme. Such was the interest generated that when it came to the vote there was more than five hundred members present in the House.

Had the vote taken place a year later, when Benjamin Disraeli was prime minister, it is very likely that Sydney and his fellow supporters of education would have been beaten. However, Gladstone was still in power and his closing speech on the matter was considered to be one which possibly altered the result of the vote. He asked the House to consider that this was a scheme of the Endowed School Commissioners. In a tone of warning, he said:

'I want to know whether the credit of the House of Commons is not engaged in the course which it is about to take in regard to this measure. You have passed, I understand, 120 schemes of the Commissioners. No attempt has been made to show — and if it were made it would entirely fail — that this scheme contains any principal whatever which has not been embodied in former schemes, unless you are ready to hold that it is a new principal if it touches the Corporation of the City of London.

'Not to vindicate the sacredness of the foundress's will, not to secure to the objects of the foundress's beneficence that which was intended for them, but for the purpose of consecrating rather negligence and wrong, and for establishing where, to say the least, there has been no special fidelity in the execution of the trust, an exceptional law, involving in its essence a principle of preference which is hateful to Englishmen, and proceeding on the principle that that which is to be applied to every other body in the country is not to be applied to the consecrated existence of the Corporation of the City of London.'

There has been no indication as to Sydney's reaction to these words given that they were spoken against the corporation in which he so fervently believed. However, in this instance, his duty was to the improvement of education and so he felt justified to take the corporation to task over this. Gladstone's speech had the required effect and the bill was carried with a slender majority of thirty-four votes.

This event then marked Sydney's twenty-year involvement with the Westminster children. He was named in the bill as one of the temporary governors of the school and, at the first meeting of the board, was elected chairman and continued in that post for another twenty years. There were actually twenty-six members of the board, but as so often happens, the main bulk of the work is done by very few, in this case it was predominantly Sydney and the vice chairman, Mr Hunt.

The transformation process of the schools was a complicated business, but it is the start and finish of the process which conveys the message best. When Sydney took charge in 1873, there were thirty boys who were boarded, clothed and educated in the old Emanuel school buildings; by 1888 there were over 850 in the new schools and the numbers never dropped below that.

The board went to work systematically, not speedily, but thoroughly. They wound up the old charities making suitable provision for the children affected. The old buildings were adapted as far as was possible, and the first school opened its doors in April 1874, just over six months after the passing of the bill. The new day school had room for 230 boys and this had been filled to capacity within two years. Under the new scheme one third of the pupils were non-fee-paying scholars, with the regular fees averaging from £4 10s per year in the lower school to £6 10s per year in the upper. Students would come from all over London although preference was given to those residing in Westminster.

As the work continued it became obvious how much of a void had been filled by the creation of the new schools. Additionally, two new day schools were built and by the end of 1876 every available space had been filled to a total of 300 boys. New buildings were erected in Palace Street, Victoria, with Sydney laying the foundation stone; these included an upper- and lower-day school, with a master's house, which was opened on 9 April 1877 by Arthur Stanley, Dean of Westminster, and which was occupied the very next day by 307 boys.

Sydney's maxim had been 'no money spent in ornament'; everything was built for educational efficiency, and experiments were conducted with schemes for paying, non-paying and part-paying scholars. As usual Sydney conducted the whole affair with his usual business-like precision. He was also very proud of the prizes and scholarships gained by his

Westminster boys. There were scholarships to Cambridge, London and Durham Universities, the Royal College of Music and King's College; some pupils were also accepted to Bart's, St Thomas', Middlesex, St Mary's and other hospitals. Boys were also taken by the Civil Service and as engineers, draughtsmen and into solicitors' offices, the railways and into City firms.

'Indeed, a boy seldom left the school without being provided with an excellent place where he had a chance to rise.'

The total cost of the school buildings had been £18,457 19s, which worked out at less than £23 for each of the 850 pupils. Sydney used to take great pleasure in comparing this to the City of London School which had been built at the same time at a cost of £70 per pupil.

The man who was appointed to run the school as its Headmaster was a Mr R. E. H. Goffin. Unfortunately, his success in the role did court a certain amount of controversy and jealousy from certain quarters. At this time there existed the *Science and Art Department*, which was a British government body promoting education in art, science, technology and design in Britain and Ireland, and was based at a large site in South Kensington in London. Because the bias of the education at Westminster was more towards science, as opposed to the arts, it was standard practice for the pupils to be entered for the 'South Kensington exams'. Goffin quickly became suspected of some underhand dealings as the pass rate by Westminster students was far higher than any other establishment in the country. One of the South Kensington officials accused Goffin of surreptitiously gaining knowledge of the contents of the examination papers, something which Goffin strongly denied. Sydney immediately appointed a special committee of enquiry which very quickly discovered that the charges were completely unfounded.

However, South Kensington would not accept the findings of the committee and refused to examine any more pupils put forward by Goffin. In response, Sydney arranged for an independent examination to be held with the result that Goffin's success rate was unchanged. Then an action was brought by the headmaster against a Colonel Donnelly, the South Kensington official who had made the original accusation. Donnelly and his superiors then pleaded privilege and there was no trial. The matter then came before the House of Commons and Sydney was persuaded to allow a select committee to be formed by Lord George Hamilton who was the vice president of the Committee of Privy Council on Education. The special committee was headed up by Robert Lowe (later Lord Sherbrooke) and its sittings were held in secret. Twenty-two witnesses from South Kensington came forward over a period of four days. Goffin was denied any counsel, was not allowed to cross-examine any of the witnesses, could not produce any witnesses of his own and was only allowed to attend when giving his own testimony. As was expected the committee upheld Donnelly's original accusation which prompted Sydney to forcibly retort:

'The result naturally confirmed in me the conviction that a parliamentary committee is the most unsatisfactory tribunal before which the guilt or innocence of a man, or the wisdom or folly of any proposition, can be considered and determined. The members of the committee are almost invariably party men, and consequently vote with the leader of their party.'

At a special meeting of the governors of the United Westminster Schools held at the Guildhall on 14 October 1879 they declined to accept the parliamentary committee's decision. It was then discovered that the government was also entitled to bring an action against Goffin and against each school governor to show cause why the headmaster should not be dismissed. The action was eventually brought with the Attorney General, Sir Henry James, appearing for the government but there were the usual delays and the whole affair threatened to drag on interminably. Finally, in order to move matters along, the school governors moved to strike the case off the record. The Attorney General, on behalf of South Kensington and the government, consented, causing the governors to urge on the court that the sole reason for the consent by the government was the lack of evidence to prove the charges against Goffin. The governors also applied for costs to be awarded in light of their accusation but this was categorically refused. Again, Sydney felt compelled to voice his opinion:

'It has been said that corporations have no consciences — have neither a soul to be saved nor a body to be kicked — and I presume governments are in the same position, and therefore think themselves justified in taking a course that would be a disgrace to any honourable man.'

Mr Goffin had been forced to incur heavy personal costs way beyond his means to enable him to fight his corner throughout the whole process. In a show of support for the headmaster, Sydney asked the charity commissioners to allow the school governors to pay the costs for Goffin; they would not. Sydney was still determined that Goffin should not be left out of pocket for the experience and discovered that under the scheme he could bypass the commissioners and get the governors to increase the grant made to the headmaster. This was duly done with an increase sufficient to cover Goffin's legal expenses.

'By this means, we were enabled to award some slight means of justice to our headmaster.'

The whole farrago had lasted almost five years and had ended with the humiliation of the South Kensington authorities and embarrassment for the government. It had shown that South Kensington never really had a case or had any justification in their hostility towards Mr Goffin. South Kensington subsequently never expressed any regret for its long and unjustified persecution of an honourable and very capable headmaster whose only fault was to be more capable than his rivals.

Upon Sydney's retirement from his post in 1893 the following address was presented to him:

'We, the assistant masters, old boys, and present boys of the United Westminster Schools, beg leave to present you with this address in commemoration of the completion of the twentieth year of the existence of the schools and your chairmanship of the Board of Governors. We recall with great satisfaction the facts—

'1. That through your strenuous exertions in Parliament and elsewhere the government of the day authorised the reconstruction of the schools on their present basis.

2. That to you as Lord Mayor of London was entrusted the duty of inaugurating the scheme proposed by the Charity Commissioners for their management and control.

3. That the governing body summoned by you in August 1873, elected you chairman of the board, and that you have been annually re-elected ever since.

'You have on many occasions been pleased to express your satisfaction at the success of the institution of which you may be justly styled the founder. We who have benefited by your exertions rejoice in this opportunity of recording our appreciation of your indefatigable energy in developing the school property, and your liberality and skill in administering the funds derived from it. But we are especially thankful to you for your unwearied zeal in the cause of education, for your active and generous sympathy with all in the schools, and for your invariable readiness to advance the prosperity of those who leave them. We trust that many years of health and happiness are before you, and that for so long a period we may be honoured with your continued friendship and guidance.'

The establishment continues in strength to this day. The main building in Palace Street, Victoria now having been expanded to meet the school's ever-growing requirements, and it continues to promote and uphold the principals laid down since its inception nearly a century and a half later. By way of further recognition of Sydney's endeavours, a copy of F.W. Taubman's statue from Waterlow Park is situated within the grounds of the school, but with one minor difference from the original...

CHAPTER XVI
WATERLOW PARK

If there could only be one place where Sydney's name is written indelibly on the map of London, it is over the twenty-nine acres in Highgate which he gave to the city, known today as Waterlow Park. The gift was made in 1889 to the London County Council, this being the local authoritative body in control at that time. However, as today, the various convolutions of the law relating to landed property were so complex that an Act of Parliament was required to make the transfer a valid proposition. In 1889 Lord Rosebery was chairman of the London County Council and so it was under his expert guidance and tact that the burdensome legal process was expedited as swiftly as possible.

By way of introduction, Sydney wrote to the LCC, the contents of which was read to the council by the chairman:

'My Dear Lord Rosebery,

'On the southern slope of Highgate Hill, in the parish of St Pancras, I own an estate of nearly 29 acres in extent, which was for many years my own home. This property, if judiciously laid out, would I think make an excellent park for the North of London.

'The grounds are undulating, well timbered with oaks, old cedars of Lebanon, and many other well-grown trees and shrubs. There are also 1½ acres of ornamental water supplied from natural springs.

'The land is freehold with the exception of 2¾ acres held on a long lease, of which thirty-five and a half years are unexpired, and it is bounded almost entirely by public roads and a public footpath.

'Commencing the work of my life as a London apprentice to a mechanical trade, I was during the whole seven years of my apprenticeship constantly associated with men of the weekly-wage class. Working shoulder to shoulder by their side, later on as a large employer of labour, and in many various other ways, I have seen much of this class and of the poorer people of London, both individually and collectively. The experience thus gained has from year to year led me more clearly to the conviction that one of the best methods for improving and elevating the social and physical condition of the working classes of this great metropolis is to provide them with decent, well-ventilated houses on self-supporting principles, and to secure for them an increased number of public parks, recreation grounds, and open spaces. This latter object can, I think, be best accomplished by the kindness of individuals acting through the agency of the London County Council, and with as little burden as possible on the public rates.

'Therefore, to assist in providing large gardens in the great city in which I have worked for fifty-three years, I desire to present to the council, as a free gift, my entire interest in the estate at Highgate above referred to.

'On the day when the conveyance is executed, and that may be as soon as your solicitors have prepared the necessary legal documents, I will in addition pay over to the council the sum of £6,000 in cash, the estimated value of the freehold interest in the 2¾ acres of leasehold, this sum of money to be used in purchasing this interest or in defraying the cost of laying out the estate as a public park in perpetuity, as the council may deem most desirable.

'If your lordship is of the opinion that this proposal is one which the members of the council are likely to accept, this letter may be communicated to them as soon as you deem expedient.'

After reading the letter, Lord Rosebery informed the council that he had visited and surveyed this beautiful piece of ground, and that he knew of no estate of the same size which had so many attractions. He told them he thought it to be a noble gift and one that was enhanced by the terms given in the letter. Sir John Lubbock (later Lord Avebury) moved for a vote of thanks to Sydney from the council for his very generous gift, this was seconded by a Mr Gibb and supported by the deputy chairman, Mr Haggis; the whole council immediately approved, although not quite with the enthusiasm one would have expected. Nevertheless, Mr Haggis did remark that the example set to the landlords of London was a grand one, and he sincerely hoped "it would prove contagious".

Whatever the official view of the London County Council may have been, the people of Highgate and surrounding areas welcomed the gesture unreservedly. They held a meeting to put their gratitude on record and resolved that:

'The gift will be of inestimable value to the large working-class population of the metropolis, and will, moreover, be highly appreciated by all classes of residents, not only on account of the historic interest of the site, but because, when taken in connection with the recently acquired Parliament Fields and Highgate Woods, it will environ a considerable proportion of Highgate with a belt of beautifully undulating land, dedicated to the public enjoyment forever.

'This meeting further recognises that, although gifts of a similar character have not been infrequent of late years in other parts of the kingdom, this is the first instance of a citizen of London giving property of this description for the use of the metropolis, where probably, from the vast aggregation of population in the Valley of the Thames, it is more needed than in any other city in the world.'

This was taking place against a London backdrop of 20,000 deaths a year being caused by the generally poor standards of sanitation, and the money being lost by this was reckoned to be £24 million per year. Mr Glover was quick to point out that Sydney clearly had a specialised knowledge of London life that allowed him to understand what the working classes would benefit from.

'They should consider the noble self-sacrifice of this gift. A man cannot part with property of this value without thinking seriously.'

Other similar meetings were held in St Pancras, Islington, Hornsey and elsewhere. The St Pancras Vestry also made a written assurance to Sydney:

'of the high regard in which he had always been held by his fellow parishioners in St Pancras, because of his long and intimate connection with the parish, his support of local charities, and his generally useful works throughout London. The Vestry trusts that he may long be spared to see with pleasure and satisfaction how greatly the people, not only of this district, but of the whole metropolis, appreciate the noble gift of what in future must be known as Waterlow Park, which in itself will be a lasting memorial of a well-spent life.'

Sydney was not the type of person who performed these acts of philanthropy in order to receive and bask in others' gratitude. To him, certainly in this instance, the greatest reward was the silent gratitude of the users of the park, of the working men and their families, the happiness of the thousands of children for whom the park was now their playground, their only playground.

On visiting the park today, a visitor cannot fail to notice F. W. Taubman's statue of Sydney with his hat and umbrella, erected as a lasting testimonial to the park's benefactor. The principal contributors to the fund for the memorial were those who lived in the neighbourhood of Highgate. The statue was unveiled by HRH Princess Louise, Duchess of Argyll; the Duke was also present and in a short speech said that on one day alone £18 had been collected from the little collection boxes which had been distributed about the park. The duke went on to say that nothing as valuable as a shilling coin had been found in the collection, and that the donations had been made up of farthings, halfpennies and pennies, testament to the fact that it was not the wealthy but rather the poorer classes who had raised this lasting monument to Sydney.

The generous benefactor was to visit the park only once more in his life. The visit was recorded by his wife, Margaret:

'It was one brilliant Saturday in August, the day before all public schools had closed for the autumn holidays, so the park was fairly overflowing with children. We drove up Highgate Hill, to what is called the Highgate Entrance; we then sent the carriage back to await us at the lower gate. Sydney had quite made up his mind to walk the full length of the park; this was an undertaking, for he was by no means strong. However, we got on slowly, and for the most part silently. He wandered about, stopping now and again at some familiar spot, remarking occasionally that he had planted this tree or that; that such an incident had occurred here or there.

'At one time, when I thought him looking tired, I suggested we should rest near where the band was playing. I remember he said emphatically: "No, I will go on. I want to hear only the voices of the children". By-and-by we came to a long straight path; there, to my surprise, I saw directly in front of us a great number of people. I hesitated for a moment, fearing an accident; then a gentleman came forward and told me that, having heard Sydney was in the park, the people had collected there in the hope of seeing him as he passed by. So we went on, and as we neared the statue the path cleared before us. And quite suddenly there went up a great shout of welcome to Sydney. There were hundreds of people and they all seemed so glad to greet him.

'His was a pathetic figure as he walked slowly along, alone, looking neither to the right nor to the left, his head uncovered, his hair in the afternoon sunshine white as snow, his figure bent, his step feeble. He was treading the old familiar path in the twilight of his life, and I could well imagine that while the children shouted, their elders were moved to many a tear.

'The whole concourse of people followed him to the lower gate, and there again, as, slowly and with an effort, he seated himself in his carriage, there went up another great shout. And then he drove away, and Sydney had parted from his old home for ever.'

CHAPTER XVII
A LIFE WELL LIVED

While wintering in their villa in Cannes in 1890, Sydney and Margaret were visited for lunch by the Prince of Wales. Sydney had a genuine respect for royalty, but this did not always extend to all the forms of deference due to the rank. To him, a king was a king, not a deity, and court ceremonies were merely that, not rituals of a higher order.

At this particular lunch Sydney happened to make a passing comment which, to others attending, some of whom may have been unaware of their host's past associations with His Royal Highness, may have appeared to be somewhat less than respectful given the company that was being kept. One of the guests expressed regret on the matter to the prince who then turned to Margaret and said:

'Lady Waterlow, I know what your husband has done to promote the happiness of the English people and the prosperity of the kingdom over which I may one day rule. Few men have done more for the poor of London, and none have asked or expected less in recognition of their services. His services have been such that I don't care what he says or omits to say to me. You may be sure I shall never take offence.'

Such was the impact of Sydney's lifetime of achievements that even a future king was happy to allow him some latitude.

Sydney and Margaret had bought the villa in Cannes as their winter home, naming it *Monterey* after the place in California where they had first met. On the advice of his doctor, Sydney spent more and more time out of London in his country home, Trosley Towers, just outside Wrotham in Kent. However, it was felt that even the Kent countryside could be a little harsh in the colder seasons for the aging man and he was ordered to seek out warmer climes for the good of his health. Sydney obliged his physician by spending October to May of each year enjoying the natural beauties of the south of France. The villa was in the Croix de Gardes quarter, at the far western end of the town. The view from the top of the hill on which it was situated had a superior view past Lord Brougham's villa to the expanse of the Mediterranean. The house itself was large, comfortable and typically British in its interior; very much a home from home.

Despite being possessed of an unenviable work ethic, Sydney was able to finally enjoy the enforced retirement due to him. He was a man who had worn an austere, rugged look throughout his life and his demeanour would appear quite severe to the outside world. He was strongly built, square in the shoulder, square in the jaw, strong-featured, the eyes full and piercing, the beard and hair growing strongly if a little ragged, and with the movement of one who would instinctively make other men step aside. Despite the external appearance, it was not long before you were able to discover that this man possessed an innate kindness within him, totally contradicting the exterior. Sydney was a man who clearly liked to have his own way, and indeed, had this not been so then the journey of Waterlow & Sons under his leadership could have been a very different story. One of his fellow directors of the Chatham and Dover Railway once said of him:

'When Sydney comes to a board meeting with his mind made up and begins to bring his heavy artillery to bear on the rest of us, there is nothing to do but get out of the way.'

So strongly did Sydney still feel about his various involvements and the need of his own counsel that he would yearly make the journey from Cannes to London in the dead of winter to attend one of many meetings, returning to France the following day. His doctors tried to prevent him from making this arduous journey but failed miserably. Even Margaret pleaded with him to consider staying at home, but he was not to be swayed. It seemed to make no difference that this would be jeopardising his health, when Sydney had his mind made up there was no other course of action to be considered.

Sydney enjoyed good conversation, but it had to be rational. If it were not logical to him, he sat in silence, regardless of the company — royalty or otherwise. He had no liking or propensity for dinner table small talk, he required a topic he could put his mind to. He was a good talker and a good listener; he liked asking questions and would expect a short, but full, answer in return.

Even in his personal life, and despite his charitable impulses, Sydney was never one to throw money away. A good friend of his was once overheard to say:

'If you want anything of Waterlow, don't ask him for a £5 note; ask him for £500 and you may get it.'

He was more than capable of small economies, as are most men whose fortunes are of their own making. He would tear off the blank half-sheets of letters and keep them in a drawer of his writing desk; he would then use one of them for that £500 gift. One of his secretaries recalled that on her first day working with him Sydney rebuked her for cutting through the string of a parcel instead of untying it. However, one such rebuke, although kindly meant, was all it took.

Often Sydney used to be asked what he considered to be the secret to his success. As was usual of the man, there was nothing forthcoming on the matter. However, he did write a piece for a periodical of the time called *The Young Man*.

'You young men must not think you have been born into the world too late, and that all the great deeds have been done, all the noble services rendered. You must not suppose that all the mighty acts of heroism have been performed, and that in your time there will be no more marching of heroes to victory and defeat; for heroes march to defeat as well as victory. Every great deed that ever was performed, or one like it, is still waiting to be performed. The weary, sad-eyed, unhappy people are still waiting, as in former times, for saviours and redeemers.

'If you fail in efforts which you may have made both earnestly and conscientiously, do not be discouraged or give way to despair; the effort is of far more consequence than the result. Always do the nearest thing to you as well as you possibly can; this is the surest way of obtaining advancement to higher class and more remunerative work. Never think for a moment that any remunerative work is beneath you. You need only be ashamed of any good work when you have not accomplished it as well as you might have done.

'If you live the right life and have faith, your reputation will be quite safe. Whatever it is that you desire for yourself, give those same things freely to others who are near you. If you wish people to speak truly to you, speak truly to them. If you wish them to love you, love them. If you want help from others, give help to all you can. Remember that it is only by giving freely of that which you most need that your own soul's wants can be supplied. Believe me, this is true.

'Never suppose or dream that the things you most covet in life can be secured by fraud, or wrong, or injustice; by lying, cowardice, or any sharp practice, or by unkindness toward your fellows, or by any evil whatsoever. You are now youths, and you may sometimes fancy that the road for you to make a start in life seems to be barred; but every day the space about you will grow wider, and if you do well with the smaller things entrusted to you, larger things will come within your grasp, and advancing years shall erelong bring you wider spheres of action, greater influences, heavier responsibilities, and deeper joys. You are the heirs of all the past ages. Be of good courage. Do not be cast down by failure or defeat, or by any sense of unworthiness. All the great men of the past sprang from such youths as you are, and the men of the future who will spring from you will do as great deeds as ever were done in the past, and they will lead lives that will shine with a lustre not less than the lustre that now shines from the lives of the great and mighty dead.'

Sydney's resignation from the position of treasurer at Bart's Hospital in 1892, followed by his resignation of the chairmanship of the Board of Governors of Westminster Schools in 1893, could be considered as the marker for the end of his long career in public service. He was strongly advised rest and a milder climate and so began to divide his time between England and the South of France. He travelled to the Riviera annually in October or November, remaining there until the following April or May; the one exception being the London directorship business visits during the winter months. While in France, Sydney took his time to enlarge and improve the villa, *Monterey*, particularly the gardens and grounds until they were among the most beautiful in Cannes. He also found a new pleasure in hospitality and in his guests. However, Cannes' social life was agreeable but exacting and Sydney took no part in it outside the confines of his own house. The socialising was left to his wife, Margaret, who was blessed with a very skilful social sense.

Many friends came to visit *Monterey* winter after winter, among them was HRH Princess Louise, the Duchess of Argyll, John Walter of *The Times* and many other notables. The business matters of the family firm gave Sydney no concern as he knew it was in safe hands, and in 1877 the chairmanship had passed to his son, Philip, who continued to nurture its growth in a very successful fashion. Another of his sons, David, became a county councillor and Member of Parliament, and Sydney also took great pleasure in later life holding earnest discussions on education with his eldest daughter, Ruth, who was for many years an active member of the London School Board.

Despite having officially retired, Sydney was still inclined to get involved with business of one sort or another, as it had the habit of finding him out; he was more than happy with this and, indeed, would have been disappointed if this had not been the case. By this stage, his health was becoming uncertain, his strength was failing, and he found himself unequal to certain tasks but nevertheless felt as if he was still in touch with current affairs. Even to the end, he had not given up all his directorships; he was still chairman of the Improved Industrial Dwellings Company, vice president of the Hospital Sunday Fund, chairman of the United Westminster Schools and director of the London, Chatham and Dover Railway. Almost his last words to his faithful servant, Hammond, were:

'Remember you call me in time Friday morning. I must go to London; there is a meeting of the Chatham and Dover.'

Whether in Cannes, London or Trosley, people still sought him out. Sydney never wished nor was rarely able to distinguish between the duties and pleasures of life and appeared incapable or unwilling to delineate between the two. Although despite this apparent practical existence, he still had time for nature and the more esoteric measures of life. He loved his gardens both at Trosley and in Cannes and would marvel in the wonder of the Mediterranean Sea and sky. One evening, while admiring the ending of the day, he observed the light shining from a single star in the evening sky. He sat for a while, taking in the sight, when finally, he spoke, "It's all very well, but who made all that?" To any ecclesiastical mind at that time, Sydney's Unitarianism was not considered a religion in its own right, but it suited his purpose well enough.

Sydney loved Trosley as he loved Villa Monterey, and for much the same reasons. Each place gave him air, space, flowers and shrubbery and, at Trosley, woods in which he had made drives which went nowhere in particular, solely to open up the wonders of the forest.

At the age of seventy-two he suffered a stroke, with a second shortly after that and the doctors had given him only a few days to live. As was typical, Sydney proved them all wrong and continued for another eleven years, and although he never re-gained his full health, few would have guessed what had befallen him.

The end came at Trosley. Only a few days previously he had been in London, and, as it was the end of July and in the height of summer, had been persuaded to return to the country where the fresh air had revived him somewhat. Three days before his death he was walking the grounds and driving in his carriage.

Margaret wrote in her journal:

'As we drove about the shady lanes there at Trosley, every time we caught sight, in the distance, of a ray of sunshine across the road, Sydney would say always the same thing: "There's sunshine beyond, my dear — there's sunshine beyond". He repeated this with so much feeling and earnestness that I cannot but believe that he felt the end was drawing near.'

Sydney died peacefully in his sleep on 3 August 1906 with his family around him. A man to be remembered as one who helped to make the world a better place than when he entered it. The epitaph he preferred to all others is his:

'Here lies one who loved his fellow-men.'

His coffin was borne on a hay cart from Trosley along the country lanes to the nearby village of Stansted, and Sydney was finally laid to rest in a quiet corner of the churchyard of St Mary the Virgin.

There would be very few people who could say that Sydney's life had not been well invested. His early years in various tough educational regimes had prepared him admirably for the rigours of life, even at such an early age. His printing apprenticeship, although arduous in itself, had played a vital role in carving out his unstinting work ethic which was to be the driving force of his achievements both personally and professionally. Sydney understood the meaning of the journey being almost more important than the destination; fortunately, in his case this was balanced equally between the two.

Sydney's business acumen could rarely be called into question. During the early days of the family firm, the introduction of a bonus scheme for the staff was something which was considered quite revolutionary. It is interesting to note that this type of incentive for a workforce is all but considered a standard working practice in our current financially acute environment. Given that all his energy appeared to be applied to the furtherance of the family business, it is remarkable that Sydney also found the time and energy to apply himself so totally to his involvement with city and national politics. This was an era when a Member of Parliament's duty had nowhere near the intensity it does today, and this enabled Sydney to more effectively balance his time to great effect. His tenure in the office of lord mayor was worthy in many respects, not least due to the introduction of more self-government for local authorities, as well as the little personal touches such as Christmas dinner for the extended family at the Mansion House.

Sydney's character and firmly held beliefs made him almost the perfect candidate for his multitude of philanthropic projects. Not wishing to undermine his outstanding work in many endeavours, it is clear that Sydney was part of a conglomerate of worthy citizens, some of whom we have heard a good deal about, some we have not, who were very focused on improving the living and working conditions of the less fortunate in society during the Victorian era. These associations extended into many projects including the treasurer's post at Bart's Hospital and his various collaborations with Florence Nightingale within that concern.

Sydney's personal life was just as colourful as his business and philanthropic adventures. As a widower, being fortunate enough to meet and marry his second wife, Margaret, having taken a chance journey to the West Coast of the United States; his various other journeys around the world incorporating Egypt, India and the Far East, something which, even by today's standards, would be considered adventurous.

It is clear that, certainly as a result of his apprenticeship and the importance of it in terms of technical education, Sydney placed great emphasis on good training for healthy employment skills. He clearly considered that 'catching them while young' was a good enough reason to champion the upgrading and development of the United Westminster Schools, and for the pupils to take that acquired knowledge on into adult life with the establishment of the City and Guilds Institute.

Even in retirement and towards the end of his life, consideration of his fellow man and his unstinting philanthropy led him to donate many acres of his own land to provide healthy recreation for the less fortunate citizens of the city he loved. It is truly a testament to this generosity that this substantial donation is still being enjoyed by the citizens of north London, and this selfless act is celebrated regularly and gladly by all those who are able to take advantage of the public park which bears his name. In further testament to this remarkable man, the land which he once owned in Kent is also now used as an area of recreation by the general public. Sydney's old home, Trosley Towers near Wrotham, was eventually demolished in the early part of the twentieth century, and the 170 acres which were the grounds of the estate have been transformed into a spectacular country park by Kent County Council as another area of natural beauty to be enjoyed by all.

A remarkable man, a remarkable life, both of which need to be remembered for the many works of selflessness performed and the legacies of which consequently remain. A testament to a very worthy member of the list of Victorian luminaries.

END